These primers on Jonathan Edwards's life a ⦚ W9-CAT-358
passion for God—provide an excellent glimp
unto God. And they help the rest of us slake our thirst for the
majesty of our Savior. We owe a great debt to Owen Strachan and
Douglas Sweeney for making Edwards and his vision of God so
accessible to the rest of us thirsty pilgrims.

> —**Thabiti Anyabwile**, Pastor of First Baptist Church of
> Grand Cayman, Cayman Islands

Everyone says Jonathan Edwards is important. Quite frankly,
however, his writing style is pretty dense by contemporary stan-
dards, so few pastors and other Christian leaders have invested
much time reading him. This new series tackles the problem.
Here is the kernel of much of Edwards's thought in eminently
accessible form.

> —**D. A. Carson**, Research Professor of New Testament,
> Trinity Evangelical Divinity School

In *The Essential Edwards Collection*, Owen Strachan and Doug
Sweeney point with knowledge and excitement to clear and
searching sections that illuminate God's truth and search our
hearts. In this collection, Edwards is introduced to a new generation of readers. His concerns are made our concerns. This is a
worthy effort and I pray that God will bless it.

> —**Mark Dever**, Senior Pastor, Capitol Hill Baptist
> Church, Washington, DC

I am deeply impressed with the vision that has brought together
this splendid library of volumes to introduce Jonathan Edwards to
a new generation. Owen Strachan and Douglas Sweeney have
provided an incredible service by making the often challenging
writings of America's greatest theologian accessible for seasoned
theologians, pastors, and students alike with their five-volume
Essential Edwards Collection. This series is properly titled the
"essential collection."

> —**David S. Dockery**, President, Union University

This series is a fantastic introduction to the heart, mind, and ministry of the greatest theologian America has ever produced.
>—**Mark Driscoll**, Pastor of Mars Hill Church, President of the Acts 29 Church Planting Network

Jonathan Edwards was a preacher of the Word, a pastor of souls, a philosopher of first rank, and the greatest theologian America has ever produced. In this wonderful new anthology of Edwards's writings, the great Puritan saint lives again. I can think of no better tonic for our transcendence-starved age than the writings of Edwards. But beware: reading this stuff can change your life forever!
>—**Timothy George**, Founding Dean of Beeson Divinity School of Samford University

Let Strachan and Sweeney serve as your guides through the voluminous writings of America's greatest theologian. They have been shaped by his godly counsel and moved by his passion for Christ. By God's grace, Edwards can do the same for you. Start your journey with *The Essential Edwards Collection*.
>—**Collin Hansen**, Author of *Young, Restless, Reformed*

Owen Strachan and Douglas Sweeney have done us all a great service by remixing and reloading the teaching of Jonathan Edwards for a new generation. They do more than introduce us to his writing: they show us how his biblical teaching relates to a modern world and leave us hungry for more. I am very impressed and very grateful for *The Essential Edwards Collection*.
>—**Joshua Harris**, Senior Pastor of Covenant Life Church

From a course he taught at Yale and in personal friendship, Doug Sweeney has taught me much about Edwards. Possessing a command of the academic field, he and Owen Strachan nevertheless write this collection with pastoral concern, showing the relevance of Edwards for our Christian faith and practice today. It's a rare combination of gifts and insights that Sweeney and Strachan bring to this task.

—**Michael Horton**, J. Gresham Machen Professor of Systematic Theology and Apologetics, Westminster Theological Seminary California

When it comes to Jonathan Edwards's writing, where does an average reader (like me!) begin? Right here, with *The Essential Edwards Collection*. Strachan and Sweeney provide a doorway into the life and teaching of one of the church's wisest theologians. The authors have also included notes of personal application to help us apply the life and teaching of Edwards to our own lives. I've read no better introduction to Jonathan Edwards.

—**C. J. Mahaney**, President of Sovereign Grace Ministries

Why hasn't this been done before? *The Essential Edwards Collection* is now essential reading for the serious-minded Christian. Doug Sweeney and Owen Strachan have written five excellent and accessible introductions to America's towering theological genius—Jonathan Edwards. They combine serious scholarship with the ability to make Edwards and his theology come alive for a new generation. *The Essential Edwards Collection* is a great achievement and a tremendous resource. I can't think of a better way to gain a foundational knowledge of Edwards and his lasting significance.

—**R. Albert Mohler Jr.**, President of The Southern Baptist Theological Seminary

A great resource! Edwards continues to speak, and this series of books is an excellent means to hear Jonathan Edwards again live and clear. Pure gold; be wise and invest in it!

—**Dr. Josh Moody**, Senior Pastor, College Church in Wheaton.

You hold in your hands a unique resource: a window into the life and thought of Jonathan Edwards, a man whose life was captured by God for the gospel of Jesus Christ. In these pages you'll not only learn about Edwards, but you'll be able to hear him speak in his own words. This winsome and accessible introduction is now the first thing I'd recommend for those who want to know more about America's greatest pastor-theologian.

—**Justin Taylor**, Managing Editor, ESV Study Bible

Jonathan Edwards is surely one of the most influential theologians of the eighteenth century. Now, at last, we have a wide-ranging and representative sample of his work published in an attractive, accessible and, most important of all, readable form. The authors are to be commended for the work they have put into this set and I hope it will become an important feature of the library of many pastors and students of the Christian faith.

—**Carl R. Trueman**, Academic Dean, Westminster Theological Seminary

JONATHAN EDWARDS
on BEAUTY

The Essential
EDWARDS
Collection

OWEN STRACHAN *and* DOUGLAS SWEENEY

MOODY PUBLISHERS
CHICAGO

© 2010 by
OWEN STRACHAN
DOUGLAS SWEENEY

All rights reserved. No part of this book may be reproduced in any form without permission in writing from the publisher, except in the case of brief quotations embodied in critical articles or reviews.

All Scripture quotations, except those that appear in original source material, are
taken from *The Holy Bible, English Standard Version.* Copyright © 2000; 2001 by
Crossway Bibles, a division of Good News Publishers. Used by permission. All rights
reserved.

Scripture quotations marked KJV are taken from the King James Version.

All websites listed herein are accurate at the time of publication, but may change in
the future or cease to exist. The listing of website references and resources does not
imply publisher endorsement of the site's entire contents. Groups, corporations, and
organizations are listed for informational purposes, and listing does not imply publisher endorsement of their activities.

Editor: Christopher Reese
Interior Design: Ragont Design
Cover Design: Gearbox

Library of Congress Cataloging-in-Publication Data

Strachan, Owen.
    Jonathan Edwards on beauty / Owen Strachan and Douglas Sweeney.
      p. cm. — (The essential Edwards collection)
    Includes bibliographical references.
    ISBN 978-0-8024-2458-7
    1. Edwards, Jonathan, 1703-1758. 2. Aesthetics—Religious aspects—
Christianity. I. Sweeney, Douglas A. II. Title.
BR115.A8S77 2009
231.7—dc22

                                                    2009040806

We hope you enjoy this book from Moody Publishers. Our goal is to provide high-
quality, thought-provoking books and products that connect truth to your real needs
and challenges. For more information on other books and products written and produced from a biblical perspective, go to www.moodypublishers.com or write to:

Moody Publishers
820 N. LaSalle Boulevard
Chicago, IL 60610

1 3 5 7 9 10 8 6 4 2

Printed in the United States of America

The Essential Edwards Collection

Jonathan Edwards: Lover of God

Jonathan Edwards on Beauty

Jonathan Edwards on Heaven and Hell

Jonathan Edwards on the Good Life

Jonathan Edwards on True Christianity

OS

To Bethany Strachan,
more beautiful than any other

DS

To Homer and Tena Hamster,
who have long known that the natural
world reflects the beauty of God

CONTENTS

Abbreviations of Works Cited   13

Foreword: Jonathan Edwards, A God-Entranced Man   15

Introduction: Entranced by God's Beauty   19

1. The Beauty of God   23

2. The Beauty of Creation   47

3. The Beauty of Christ   71

4. The Beauty of the Church   97

5. The Beauty of the Trinitarian Afterlife   119

Conclusion: Beauty Remembered   141

Acknowledgments   145

Recommended Resources on Jonathan Edwards   147

Abbreviations of Works Cited

The following shortened forms of books by or about Jonathan Edwards are used in the text to indicate the source of quotations.

Books in the Yale University Press
Works of Jonathan Edwards series

In the text, the volumes are listed in the following format: (*Works* 1, 200). The "1" refers to the series volume; the "200" refers to the page number in the given volume.

Edwards, Jonathan. *Scientific and Philosophical Writings*, ed. Wallace E. Anderson, *The Works of Jonathan Edwards*, vol. 6. New Haven: Yale, 1980.

_____. *Ethical Writings*, ed. Paul Ramsay, *The Works of Jonathan Edwards*, vol. 8. New Haven: Yale, 1989.

_____. *A History of the Work of Redemption*, ed. John F. Wilson, *The Works of Jonathan Edwards*, vol. 9. New Haven: Yale, 1989.

_____. *Sermons and Discourses, 1720–1723*, ed. Wilson Kimnach, *The Works of Jonathan Edwards*, vol. 10. New Haven: Yale, 1992.

_____. *Typological Writings*, ed. Wallace E. Anderson and David Watters, *The Works of Jonathan Edwards*, vol. 11. New Haven: Yale, 1993.

_____. *Notes on Scripture*, ed. Stephen Stein, *The Works of Jonathan Edwards*, vol. 15. New Haven: Yale, 1998.

_____. *Letters and Personal Writings*, ed. George S. Claghorn, *The Works of Jonathan Edwards*, vol. 16. New Haven: Yale, 1998.

_____. *Sermons and Discourses, 1730–1733*, ed. Mark Valeri, *The Works of Jonathan Edwards*, vol. 17. New Haven: Yale, 1999.

_____. *Sermons and Discourses, 1734–1738*, ed. M. X. Lesser, *The Works of Jonathan Edwards*, vol. 19. New Haven: Yale, 2001.

_____. *Sermons and Discourses, 1739–1742*, ed. Harry S. Stout and Nathan O. Hatch with Kyle P. Farley, *The Works of Jonathan Edwards*, vol. 22. New Haven: Yale, 2003.

Jonathan Edwards, a God-Entranced Man

*W*hen I was in seminary, a wise professor told me that besides the Bible I should choose one great theologian and apply myself throughout life to understanding and mastering his thought. This way I would sink at least one shaft deep into reality, rather than always dabbling on the surface of things. I might come to know at least one system with which to bring other ideas into fruitful dialogue. It was good advice.

The theologian I have devoted myself to is Jonathan Edwards. All I knew of Edwards when I went to seminary was that he preached a sermon called "Sinners in the Hands of an Angry God," in which he said something about hanging over hell by a slender thread. My first real encounter with Edwards was when I read his "Essay on the Trinity" and wrote a paper on it for church history.

It had a lasting effect on me. It gave me a conceptual framework with which to grasp, in part, the meaning of saying God is three in one. In brief, there is God the Father, the fountain of being, who from all eternity has had a perfectly clear and distinct image and idea of himself; and this image is the eternally begotten Son. Between this Son and Father there flows a stream of infinitely vigorous love and perfectly holy communion; and this is God the Spirit. God's Image of God and God's Love of God are so full of God that they are fully divine Persons, and not less.

After graduation from college, and before my wife and I took off for graduate work in Germany, we spent some restful days on a small farm in Barnesville, Georgia. Here I had another encounter with Edwards. Sitting on one of those old-fashioned two-seater swings in the backyard under a big hickory tree, with pen in hand, I read *The Nature of True Virtue*. I have a long entry in my journal from July 14, 1971, in which I try to understand, with Edwards's help, why a Christian is obligated to forgive wrongs when there seems to be a moral law in our hearts that cries out against evil in the world.

Later, when I was in my doctoral program in Germany, I encountered Edwards's *Dissertation Concerning the End for Which God Created the World*. I read it in a pantry in our little apartment in Munich. The pantry was about 8 by 5 feet, a most unlikely place to read a book like the *Dissertation*. From my perspective now, I would say that if there were one book that captures the essence or wellspring of Edwards's theology, this would be it. Edwards's answer to the question of why God created the world is this: to emanate the fullness of His glory for His people to know, praise, and enjoy. Here is the heart of his theology in his own words:

> IT APPEARS THAT ALL that is ever spoken of in the Scripture as an ultimate end of God's works is included in that one phrase, *the glory of God.* In the creatures' knowing, esteeming, loving, rejoicing in and praising God, the glory of God is both exhibited and acknowledged; his fullness is received and returned. Here is both the *emanation* and *remanation.* The refulgence shines upon and into the creature, and is reflected back to the luminary. The beams of glory come from God, and are something of God and are refunded back again to their original. So that the whole is *of* God and *in* God, and *to* God, and God is the beginning, middle and end in this affair.

That is the heart and center of Jonathan Edwards and, I believe, of the Bible too. That kind of reading can turn a pantry into a vestibule of heaven.

I am not the only person for whom Edwards continues to be a vestibule of heaven. I hear testimonies regularly that people have stumbled upon this man's work and had their world turned upside down. There are simply not many writers today whose mind and heart are God-entranced the way Edwards was. Again and again, to this very day his writings help me know that experience.

My prayer for *The Essential Edwards Collection* is that it will draw more people into the sway of Edwards's God-entranced worldview. I hope that many who start here, or continue here, will make their way to Edwards himself. Amazingly, almost everything he wrote is available on the Internet. And increasingly his works are available in affordable books. I am thankful that Owen Strachan and Douglas Sweeney share my conviction that every effort to point to Edwards, and through him to his God, is a worthy investment of our lives. May that be the outcome of these volumes.

> John Piper
> Pastor for Preaching and Vision
> Bethlehem Baptist Church
> Minneapolis, Minnesota

*Entranced by
God's Beauty*

*T*here is something about the face of a happy, smiling child that calls to a deeper part of a person's soul. Something beyond triteness and the mundane. Something pure and clear. Something that reaches out to the beholder and urges him or her to enjoy this moment, to capture it in their mind, and to recall it over and over again. What is this quality? What calls us with such force to adore and enjoy simple things like a child's smile?

Surely it is beauty. Hard to describe but easy to identify, beauty resides in expected and unexpected places in our world. Many would cite famous celebrities as exemplars of physical beauty. Others would think of a far-away locale like a tropical island. Still others would note that beauty is not merely physical, but is present in kind-hearted actions and pleasing dispositions. Selfless sacrifice would fit this category, or racial unification. As is clear from even a few examples, beauty is present in our world in a variety of forms.

Yet, while the average person might think about the reality of beauty from time to time, few people would think about the source of beauty. Where does beauty come from? Why is it here? How are we to figure out its origin in a world that is full of unbeautiful things and acts—crimes, blights, and pain? When one considers just how much evil is committed in a single day by the world's inhabitants, beauty seems fragile and transient. Perhaps beauty can dry up, and fade away? Perhaps there is no source, and beauty is merely a pleasing product of a cosmic game of chance? These and other questions confront those who seek to know the source of beauty.

Several hundred years ago, the Northampton pastor Jonathan Edwards did some thinking of his own on this difficult subject. Possessing a taste for beauty from an early age, Edwards thought deeply about the source and nature of true beauty in a sin-cursed world. Over the course of his pastoral career in a small New England town, Edwards returned to the subject again and again, threading it into his sermons, notes, and theological writings. Though few people would think of Edwards as a man captivated by the very idea of beauty, he was. This volume will explore his meditation on the subject and lay out a Christian framework for understanding and experiencing the beauty God has planted in His world.

Yet this book must go beyond the theological study of aesthetics, as Edwards himself did. The pastor did not merely pose and answer questions about beauty. He found in his study of beauty the person of God. In other words, where Edwards saw beautiful images and acts, he saw a representation, a small picture, of a reality too great to fully comprehend. The study of true beauty was for Edwards the study of God. In this devotional pursuit, Edwards found rich and perpetual food for his soul. He discovered nothing less than the purpose of his life and the meaning of his existence. His life was to be a reflection of the beauty of God, a small mirror catching and sending back the rays of the Lord's divinity, winning Him glory and honor until life on earth closed and life in heaven began.

The Lord had in fact crafted a great plan by which to express His beauty and make His glory known. He existed as the resplendent one, but did not content Himself with mere self-appreciation of His beauty. Instead, He set in motion an arc of glory that began with Himself, moved to the creation, continued with the incarnation of Christ, moved next to the church, the bride of Christ, and is consummated in heaven, where the Holy Trinity dwells. It is this arc, this chain, that the book traces, devoting a chapter to each of these points in the great chain of events.

We present this subject matter by interacting with the actual writing of Edwards. It will take a little time to get used to his style, but it is our belief that investing even a little effort in reading his writing will yield a huge spiritual payoff. His meditations are so deep, so thoughtful, and so fresh that we are confident that you will profit from them if you give them a chance. There are few resources in the Christian world so rich as the Edwards corpus. We will splice in our commentary on his writing even as we sketch a general picture of his views on beauty. As we go, we will offer brief suggestions for application of his views that we hope will be of use to you in your personal reading or in the context of group study.

Though we both enjoy delving deeply into subjects like this one, we cannot cover every base in this book. The additional volumes in the *Essential Edwards Collection* allow the reader to delve much deeper into his thinking and preaching, but we seek in *Jonathan Edwards on Beauty* to bring to light a central tenet of Edwards's thought, one often overlooked but filled with rich discoveries. This book is intended for the uninitiated, but we hope and intend for it—and for this series —to be of use to pastors, students, church leaders, small groups, and many more besides.

Let us dive into this short book, then, with this central idea fixed in our mind: in all that was good, and true, and virtuous, in all that was aesthetic and pure, Edwards found shimmers and reflections of His God. Far from a momentary glance at nature through the window, life was one long enterprise in treasuring the beauty of God, an endeavor that took its starting point from the vision of God set forth in Holy Scripture. To live for this God, to know the beauty of redeemed life with Him, was to truly live. In the pages that follow, we will unpack this insight and experience through study of Edwards's writings the quest for beauty that consumed an eighteenth-century pastor and that will do the same for us today.

CHAPTER 1

The Beauty of God

*W*hat is the starting point of Christian faith? When you wake up and begin your morning study of the Bible, what are you seeking to find out? Or, to go back in time a bit, why did you begin to study the Bible in the first place?

The starting point of religion or spirituality for many today is the individual and his or her subjective feelings. What do I want? What do I need, in a spiritual sense? How can religion, and whatever superpower lies behind it, serve me and meet my desires? In short, what can I get from this deal? Sadly, even Christians are not immune to these questions.

Though biblical spirituality certainly addresses and responds to the heart-cries of lost sinners, its starting point is nothing other than the living God. From the awe-inspiring opening of Genesis 1:1—"In the beginning God"—to the cataclysmic ending of Revelation 21:22—"in the city . . . is the Lord God the Almighty and the Lamb"—the Bible declares without interruption or apology that God is the starting and ending points of true religion. As portrayed in the Bible, God does not bow to man. Man, lost and helpless, bows to God.

The great New England pastor and theologian Jonathan Edwards seized upon this central truth early in his life. When he was a young, budding scholar at Yale University, he suddenly discovered in his daily meditation on the Scripture "a sense of the glory of the divine being" that transformed his life (*Works* 16, 492). Reflecting later on this chrysalis moment, Edwards preached that with genuine faith "There is not only a speculatively judging that God is gracious, but a sense how amiable God is upon that account, or a sense of the beauty of this divine attribute" (*Works* 17, 413). When a sinner comes to understand the graciousness of God, and the majesty of His character, they see with piercing clarity that "There is a divine and superlative glory in these things; an excellency that is of a vastly higher kind, and more sublime nature than in other things; a glory greatly distinguishing them from all that is earthly and temporal" (*Works* 17, 413). In this chapter, we examine the center of Edwards's theology, the Lord God, who formed the first link in a cycle of beauty that begins with creation and runs its course to heaven.

The Starting Point of Theology

When the young Yale tutor pushed past the muddle of everyday life and became aware of God's ineffable character, it was as if scales fell from his eyes. The theater, the cosmic drama, of God's reign over the world came into view, and Jonathan stood transfixed. He saw heaven and hell, man and Satan, in clearer view than ever before. But above all, Jonathan saw the Lord. He knew then that God was no abstract deity, but was a personal being whom all creation could not contain. In his sermon "God's Excellencies," preached in 1720, the same year of his spiritual breakthrough, Jonathan considered the qualities of God that robed Him in splendor. He prefaced his analysis with a warning of his unworthiness for the task:

WHAT POOR, MISERABLE CREATURES, then, are we, to talk of the infinite and transcendent gloriousness of the great, eternal, and almighty Jehovah; what miserable work do worms of the dust make, when they get upon such a theme as this, which the very angels do stammer at? But yet, although we are but worms and insects, less than insects, nothing at all, yea, less than nothing, yet so has God dig- nified us, that he has made [us] for this very end: to think and be astonished [at] his glorious perfections. And this is what we hope will be our business to all eternity; to think on, to delight [in], to speak of, and sing forth, the infinite excellencies of the Deity. He has made us capable of understanding so much of him here as is necessary in order to our acceptable worshipping and praising him, and he has instructed us, and taught us, as little ignorant babes and infants, and has helped our weak understanding by his instructions; he has told us what he is, has condescended to our poor capacities and described himself to us after the manner of men: as men, when they teach children, must teach them after their manner of thinking of things, and come down to their childish capacities, so has God taught us concerning himself. (*Works* 10, 417–18)

The one who spoke of God, in Edwards's mind, did so as a created, lowly being, a "worm of the dust." This is a striking beginning for the study of God. One did not discuss the Lord as an abstract concept. One begins the study of theology lying in the dust beside the prophet Ezekiel, heart pounding, eyes straining to shut out the piercing glory of God (Ezekiel 1:28–2:10).

Beginning his study of God with the Word of God, Edwards, like Ezekiel, raised himself from the ground and began to speak of what he saw. God's beauty had numerous facets and required all man's senses to comprehend it. Edwards identified seven attributes that demonstrated God's excellency, or beauty. Edwards's descriptions of these are worth quoting at length. One should ponder them slowly and meditatively, for they provide rich food for one's spiritual nourishment.

Eternality and Self-Existence

The first of these was longevity and independence of existence. Edwards strove to wrap his mind around the reality that God had always existed. He wrote:

[I]T IS NECESSARY THAT that which hath a beginning must have some cause, some author that gave it a beginning, but God never had a beginning; there was none before him, and therefore none that gave him his being. He thanks no one for his being; doth not, nor ever did depend upon any for it, but receives his being from himself, and depends alone on himself. Neither doth he thank anyone for anything he enjoys: his power, his wisdom, his excellency, his glory, his honor, and [his] authority are his own, and received from none other; he possesses them and he will possess them: he is powerful and he will be powerful; he is glorious and he will be glorious; he is infinitely honorable, but he receives his honor from himself; he is infinitely happy and he will be infinitely happy; he reigns and rules over the whole universe, and he will rule and do what he pleases, in the armies of heaven and amongst the inhabitants of the earth. Poor nothing creatures can do nothing towards controlling of [Him]; they, with all their power conjoined, which is but weakness, can't deprive Jehovah of any of these things. He was just the same, in all respects, from all eternity as he is now; as he was, infinite ages before the foundations of the world were laid, so he is now and so he will be, with exactly the same glory and happiness uninterrupted, immovable and unchangeable, the same yesterday, today, and forever. (*Works* 10, 419)

As Edwards saw Him, God dwelt in a realm of glory untouched by time and age, dependent on nothing for His timeless existence. Theologians use the term aseity to describe the utter independence and power of God. God "thanks no one for his being," as Edwards put it. His existence is underived. He is altogether powerful, needing no one, never aging, never changing, never growing weary. From the beginning of time until the end of the universe, God exists.

One of the central ironies of the Christian life is that the more we come to learn about God, the more awesome He appears. No matter how high-powered one's mind may be, He is the "immovable and unchangeable" one, a timeless figure from a realm outside our own. Finite creatures simply cannot comprehend His duration of existence, hard as we try. The more we understand, the more we realize how little we truly know.

Greatness

God's greatness, or exalted status, stands beside His length of existence as a second element of His excellency. Over every living thing, Edwards preached, stands God:

> GOD IS INFINITELY EXALTED above all created beings in
> greatness. This earth appears to us as a very great thing.
> When we think of the large countries and continents, the
> vast oceans, and the great distance between one country
> and another, the whole, together, appears very great and
> vast; but especially doth the great universe surprise us with
> its greatness, to which, without doubt, this vast earth, as we
> call it, is less than any mote or dust, that ever we saw, is to
> the whole earth; but how shall we be surprised when we
> think that all this vast creation, making the most of it we
> can, is infinitely less, when compared with the greatness of
> God, than the least discernible atom is to the whole cre-
> ation! (*Works* 10, 419)

Over all the heights of the universe stands the Lord God.
There is no point of comparison between God and all else,
wrote Edwards; He "is infinitely exalted above all." God has no
end, and one cannot map out His coordinates. He is vast and
mysterious, greater than the greatest things we can imagine.
His scope speaks to His majestic beauty.

Loveliness

The third attribute that shows God's beauty is His loveliness or splendor. Edwards used picturesque images to
describe God's bountiful loveliness:

THE BEAUTY OF TREES, plants, and flowers, with which
God has bespangled the face of the earth, is delightful; the
beautiful frame of the body of man, especially in its perfection, is astonishing; the beauty of the moon and stars is
wonderful; the beauty of [the] highest heavens is transcendent; the excellency of angels and the saints in light is very
glorious: but it is all deformity and darkness in comparison
of the brighter glories and beauties of the Creator of all, for
"behold even to the moon, and it shineth not" (Job 25:5);
that is, think of the excellency of God and the moon will
not seem to shine to you, God's excellency so much out-
shines [it]. And the stars are not pure in his sight, and so we
know that at the great day when God appears, the sun shall
be turned into darkness, shall hide his face as if he were
ashamed to see himself so much outshined; and the very
angels, they hide their faces before him; the highest heavens are not clean in his sight, and he charges his angels
with folly. (*Works* 10, 421)

While a pastor in Northampton, Massachusetts (1726–1750),
Edwards loved to take long walks or ride his horse through
the stunning New England countryside. Though he relished
the outdoors, he knew that the beauty of the earth was nothing but a passing shadow compared to the beauty of God. The
shining stars and the brisk Northampton nights, though grand,
were still "not pure in his sight." Even the very realm of the

Lord, "the highest heavens," pale in comparison to Him. God's beauty is perfect, and all appears unclean in comparison.

Power

The fourth attribute that displayed the beauty of God was His power. Over the most powerful people of the earth, God reigned as King:

> WHEN HE PLEASES, one king must die, and who he pleases must reign in his room; armies conquer or are conquered according as he will have it: "The king's heart is in the hand of the Lord, and he turns them as the rivers of water" [Proverbs 21:1]. Thus he holds an absolute and uncontrollable government in the world; and thus he has done from the beginning, and thus he will do to the end of all things. Neither is his dominion confined to the children of men, but he rules the whole creation. He gives commands to the seas, and has appointed them bounds which they cannot pass; "which removeth the mountains, and they know it not who overturneth them in his anger; which shaketh the earth out of its place, and the pillars thereof tremble; who commandeth the sun and it riseth not; who sealeth up the stars, which maketh Arcturus and Orion, and the chambers of the south; who doth great things past finding out; yea, wonders without number" [Job 9:5-7, Job 9:9-10]. (*Works* 10, 422)

Edwards summarized this material by noting:

> WHAT A VAST and uncontrollable dominion hath the
> almighty God. The kings of the earth are not worthy of the
> name, for they are not able to execute their authority in
> their narrow bounds, except by the power and assistance of
> their subjects, but God rules most absolutely the whole
> universe by himself; kings rule, perhaps sometimes for forty
> years, but God's kingdom is an everlasting kingdom, and of
> his dominion there is no end. Well, therefore, may he be
> said to be the blessed and only potentate, King of Kings,
> and Lord of Lords. (*Works* 10, 422)

Over against the self-importance of earthly rulers, Edwards
asserted the sovereignty of the God of the Bible. Kings
thought that they governed with unchallenged authority, but
Edwards's God "rules the whole creation," "gives commands
to the seas," and oversees "most absolutely the whole universe
by himself" while He advances His "everlasting kingdom."
The Lord controls the hearts of men but is Himself "uncontrollable." The power of this God is itself a work of beauty, an
aesthetic performance. In the hurricane's squall, the shuddering of the earth, the eruption of a volcano, we glimpse the
force that formed this world and rules over it until the end of
the age.

Wisdom

The fifth element of God's excellence and beauty is His wisdom. Edwards turned again to the best of human beings to compare them to God:

> THE WISEST OF MEN, how little do they know, how fre-quently are they deceived and frustrated, and their wisdom turned to foolishness, their politic designs undermined; but when was the time that God's wisdom failed, that he did not obtain his end, although all the bleak army of hell are continually endeavoring to counterwork him? When was it that God altered his mind and purpose, or took a wrong step in the government of the world? (*Works* 10, 423)

Edwards revealed that God's purposes are not frustrated. What He plans according to His stores of wisdom, He does. The earth and all who live in it take their cues from Him. He is quite unlike even "the wisest of men," who cannot help but see "their wisdom turned to foolishness" and their "politic designs undermined." God may face resistance to His plans, but only for so long as He tolerates it. No man can stand before Him, and no one can resist His will (Romans 9:19).

Edwards believed strongly in the infallibility of God, His inability to make an error or mistake of any kind. God's infi-nite knowledge undergirded this trait:

SOLOMON WAS SENSIBLE that there was need of uncommon and extraordinary wisdom to rule such a kingdom as he had; but what wisdom, what vast knowledge and infinite penetration must he have, who has every being in the world to rule and govern; who rules every thought, and every purpose, every motion and action, not only of angels and men, but of every creature, great and small, even to every little atom in the whole creation, and that forever and ever? What infinite wisdom and knowledge is necessary and requisite in order to this! But this God doth; this he hath done and will do. All the changes and alterations that happen in all the world, heaven and earth, whether great or never so small, he knows it altogether, even to the least insect that crawls upon the earth, or dust that flies in the air, and it is all from his disposal, and according to his eternal determination. (*Works* 10, 423)

Edwards compared the Lord to Solomon, the wisest man who ever lived. Solomon, Edwards noted, used his intelligence and discernment "to rule such a kingdom as he had," but God "rules every thought, and every purpose, every motion and action" of all that will ever live and breathe on the earth. To reign wisely, Solomon collected whatever knowledge he could; God, however, possesses all the knowledge of the world without sending so much as a solitary angel from heaven to report back. In Edwards's simple phrase, "He knows it altogether."

The knowledge of God extends over and into all things. The Lord is by definition not a limited, finite being like a human. He knows all and exercises complete control over all. If it were not so, Edwards's words indicate, He would not be God.

God's Beauty: Holiness

The sixth quality of God that rendered Him beautiful in the mind of the Massachusetts theologian was His holiness. "Now God is infinitely holy," Edwards declared:

AND INFINITELY EXALTED THEREIN, above the holy angels and all creatures; there is not the least tincture of defilement or pollution in the Deity, but he is infinitely far from it: he is all pure light, without mixture of darkness; he hates and abhors sin above all things, 'tis what is directly contrary to his nature. This, his great holiness, has he made known to us by his justice, truth, and faithfulness in all his dispensations towards us, and by the pure holiness of his laws and commands.

Holiness used to be for a distinguishing attribute between the God of Israel and other gods, Daniel 4:8, "But at last Daniel came in before me, whose name is Belteshazzar, according to the name of my God, and in whom is the spirit of the holy gods"; and so in the next verse, "because I know the holy gods is in thee." Likewise, in the

eighteenth verse, "the Holy One" is a name that God seems
to delight [in]. 'Tis that attribute which continually ravishes
the seraphims, and causes them continually to cry in their
praises, without ceasing, "holy, holy, holy." This is the sound
with which the highest heaven, the palace of God, perpetually rings, and [it] will ring on earth in the glorious times
that are hastening. (*Works* 10, 423–4)

Above the greatest, purest beings one could conceive, the
Lord shone in the mind of Edwards and the world beyond "in
the splendor of his holiness" (Psalm 96:9). Using one of his
favorite metaphors, Edwards preached that the Lord "is all
pure light, without mixture of darkness." As with so much of
Edwards's discussion of the Lord's attributes, moral and ethical description mingles with aesthetic and physical description. The Lord's appearance relates directly to His works even
as His works relate directly to His appearance. He does that
which is of the light, and He Himself is the light. His character, like His person, radiates. His holiness is the spark that
illuminates the heavens and the earth.

Goodness

The seventh and final attribute described by Edwards as
a part of God's overarching excellence was His goodness. This
attribute consisted primarily of a blend of kindness and justice
that God frequently manifested to the world:

GOD IS INFINITELY EXALTED above all created beings in goodness. Goodness and royal bounty, mercy, and clemency is the glory of earthly monarchs and princes, but in this is the Lord, our God, infinitely exalted above them. God delights in the welfare and prosperity of his creatures; he delights in making of them exceeding happy and blessed, if they will but accept of the happiness which he offers.

All creatures do continually live upon the bounty of God; he maintains the whole creation of his mere goodness: every good thing that is enjoyed is a part of his bounty. When kings are bountiful, and dispense good things to their subjects, they do but give that which the Almighty before gave to them. So merciful and so full of pity is God, that when miserable man, whom He had no need of, who did Him no good, nor could be of any advantage to Him, had made himself miserable by his rebellion against God, He took such pity on him that He sent His only Son to undergo his torment for him, that he might be delivered and set free. And now He offers freely, to bestow upon those rebels, complete and perfect happiness to all eternity upon this, His Son's account. There never was such an instance of goodness, mercy, pity, and compassion since the world began; all the mercy and goodness amongst creatures fall infinitely short of it: this is goodness that never was, never will, never can be paralleled by any other beings. (*Works* 10, 424)

Edwards compared the potent goodness of God with the goodness of the most powerful earthly figure, the king. His comparison showed how much greater God was than even the most majestic emperor. The king could show "bounty, "mercy," and "clemency," but all his goodness paled before the supernatural kindness of the Lord.

In Edwards's conception, God's goodness meant that "he delights in making" His people "exceeding happy and blessed." The highest expression of this goodness was the crucifixion of the Son of God. In the death of Jesus Christ, God showed His kindness and love to sinners on a scale only infinity could contain. "There never was such an instance of goodness, mercy, pity, and compassion," Edwards asserted, for "this is goodness that never was, never will, never can be paralleled by any other beings." No one else could qualify to take on the sins of mankind, bear the wrath of God, and cleanse the guilty but the Son of God. One could spot God's goodness in countless forms throughout the world—whether in His general care for mankind or His special care for His people—but nowhere in greater measure than in the death of Jesus Christ.

The beauty of God was, in the eyes of Edwards, a multifaceted diamond, a precious collection of attributes in their purest form: self-existence, greatness, loveliness, power, wisdom, holiness, and goodness. Over all the earth and all the created order stood this Lord, beautiful for the perfections of His person. Edwards discovered these perfections in Scripture and thus began his spiritual life and theological thought from a God-centered starting point.

Making God's Beauty Known

Because of His majesty, unfolded in the seven attributes examined above, the Lord properly delighted in Himself and the mere presence of His own beauty. Before one discussed creation, or Christ's incarnation, or the church, or heaven, one had to realize that God's self-sufficiency, His perfect fullness and majesty, rendered Him the only figure in existence who could justly glory in and be satisfied by Himself. Edwards articulated this foundational point in his 1749 work *Dissertation Concerning the End for Which God Created the World*, where he argued that:

GOD'S LOVE TO HIMSELF, and his own attributes, will therefore make him delight in that which is the use, end and operation of these attributes. If one highly esteem and delight in the virtues of a friend, as wisdom, justice, etc., that have relation to action, this will make him delight in the exercise and genuine effects of these virtues: so if God both esteem and delight in his own perfections and virtues, he can't but value and delight in the expressions and genuine effects of them. So that in delighting in the expressions of his perfections, he manifests a delight in his own perfections themselves: or in other words, he manifests a delight in himself; and in making these expressions of his own perfections his end, *he makes himself his end.* (Works 8, 437)

Edwards elaborated on this point, developing the idea that God's focal point in His existence was the enjoyment of His own glory:

> THE MORAL RECTITUDE of God's heart must consist in a proper and due respect of his heart to things that are objects of moral respect: that is, to intelligent beings capable of moral actions and relations. And therefore it must chiefly consist in giving due respect to that Being to whom most is due; yea, infinitely most, and in effect all. For God is infinitely and most worthy of regard. (*Works* 8, 421–22)

The essence of this section is that God's majestic nature not only enables but calls Him to glory in Himself. As a perfect being, a figure of absolute eternality, greatness, loveliness, power, wisdom, holiness, and goodness, God deserved to celebrate and glorify Himself. This assertion of Edwards intensifies one's understanding of the beauty and worth of God. Because of His excellent nature, God is wholly justified in seeking glory and honor and praise and worship for Himself. This is the foundation for Edwards's entire theological system, and it shapes his view of creation, Christ, the church, and heaven, as subsequent chapters will show.

Edwards's treatment of the traits of God offers a framework by which to comprehend and approach the Lord. God alone is self-sufficient and worthy of worship. Writing three hundred years ago, Edwards illuminated this fundamental reality of Scripture and showed that God, possessing beauty beyond human comprehension, is the only being deserving of worship. We began our study in the dust, like the prophet Ezekiel, and we end like another Old Testament figure, Moses, coming down from the mountain with faces shining from the glory of God we have just glimpsed.

 *Pursuing Beauty*

The Necessity of Humility

*I*n the current day, we are taught by many writers and preachers, religious or otherwise, to begin our spiritual quests, our faith journeys, with ourselves. We are encouraged to seek God because He can meet our needs and satisfy our deepest desires. There is some truth to this claim, but the fundamental duty of every person before the holy God is to humble themselves (Ecclesiastes 12:13). Unlike what certain leaders tell us, we do not come to God and begin articulating a list of deep-seated desires and needs. If we have biblical faith, we must fall before our majestic God, trembling to be in His presence, rejoicing that because of the blood of Christ we have access to Him and will not be crushed by the weight of His glory. If we have been taught that religion is all about us, if we find ourselves breathing the "me-centered" air of our day, then we must cleanse ourselves, reorient our minds, and approach God in a new way.

Because God is God, He must first be honored and treasured and reverenced. In our hearts, we must follow Edwards as he follows various biblical figures, and humble ourselves before the Lord (2 Chronicles 7:14, for example). In doing so, we will truly care for ourselves. In dying to ourselves, we will live to Christ (Philippians 1:20). We need not reject concern for our souls and our eternal good, but we do need to rightly focus that concern upon a righteous, holy God.

This will mean that we may have to make some changes in our spiritual lives. Some of the books that we read, the preachers that we listen to, the things that we've learned to tell ourselves, we must set aside. We must take practical steps in our self-centered world to embrace the radically biblical truth that life is about God first, and then about us. We are not Him, and we must not live as such. True knowledge of God begins with humility, quietness before the Lord, and a willingness to listen to God's Word and to order our lives according to it (Proverbs 1:7). Only when we possess and practice this mindset can we fully appreciate the beauty of the One who in His mercy has claimed us through the death and resurrection of His Son and the regeneration of His Spirit.

Applying the Knowledge of God to Our Lives

*T*he study of God's attributes provides nearly endless fuel for the daily life of the Christian. Contrary to what many think, these doctrines are not dry or lifeless, but packed with spiritual food by which to nourish our lives. It would help to take considerable chunks of time to think about each of the seven attributes of God explored by Edwards in his priceless sermon. Meditating on and applying each attribute to real-life situations will transform our daily lives. We may not be able to change all of the circumstances that affect us, but we can make our lives beautiful as we study the beauty of the God we serve.

There are many applications of the seven attributes of God to our lives. The fact that God is eternal can give us great encouragement as our lives hurry on (Revelation 22:13). Reigning over us is a timeless God who holds each moment of our lives in His hands and who has planned each of them to give Him glory in some way. Pondering this reality can free us from anxiety as we realize that the Lord has counted each of our days and is using them for His purpose. Remembering His timelessness will calm us and restrain us from a frenetic pattern of life.

The Lord is great (Psalm 96). Though it can be initially puzzling to think about how God's grandeur applies to our lives, we can find incredible comfort in this fact. God is not small, He is not limited. He is limitless. He is majestic. We are small and finite. Even the most fleeting recognition of this reality can free us from pride. Compared to the living God, what is the wisest person, the strongest athlete, the scariest enemy? Remembering this will cause us to rein in our natural arrogance and to worship the great God of heaven and earth.

Our God is lovely (Psalm 90:17). His beauty is undimmed. Nothing can or will change this aspect of His nature. Though we are so often tempted by beautiful things on this earth, we believers have been claimed by a being far more beautiful and lovely than anything in creation. We have not of course seen God in person, but we have seen His character, and read of His splendor, and discovered His excellent Son, and these vistas can lift us from giving in to temptation to lesser things if we simply raise our vision on a regular basis to behold the beauty of the Lord.

The Creator is powerful (Psalm 93). He is the only one who truly deserves the title *awesome*. His strength, like His scope, is limitless. He can do whatever He pleases. Contemplating this trait will enable us to claim strength in areas where we are weak and to find release from self-dependency. Sooner or later, our strength will fail. We will inevitably and repeatedly lose the ability to control our lives and create good for ourselves and our loved ones. How helpful it will be for us to think about the might of God and to allow our understanding and of this strength to shape the way we live our lives in dependence on the Lord.

The Lord is wise (Proverbs 2). Over all the false wisdom that we trust, and over all the foolish thinking we think is wise, the wisdom of the Lord is right and true. In a world where so many clamor for our allegiance, we must remember that only the Lord is truly wise. Our hearts are calibrated by our sinful natures to stray from Him and His wisdom. We cannot forget this reality, and we need to constantly read Scripture to come into contact with divine wisdom and to keep ourselves from embracing folly.

The Most High is holy (1 Samuel 2:2). He is spotless and pure. He has no blemish, and none can find fault with Him. As the Lord is holy, so are we called to be holy (1 Peter 1:13–16). The chief way to become holy is not to start out by following a list of rules, but to examine the Lord's character, to know His Word, and to follow the example of His Son. The local church will help us greatly in learning what it means to be holy, for there we find people who are living holy lives not to check off legalistic boxes, but to present their entire beings as a thank offering to God. How crucial, then, that we join and become active members in our local churches, where we can learn God's Word and encourage one another to conform our lives to it.

Our heavenly Father, finally, is good (Psalm 135:3). His goodness extends throughout our lives. Perhaps the best way to apply the doctrine of God's goodness is to live a perpetually thankful life (1 Thessalonians 5:18). In so doing we will honor Him who gave His Son for us—the greatest expression of mercy and kindness the world has ever known.

Meditation on these attributes is meant to provide fuel for faith and love of God. Every Christian would do well to consider them in personal devotions and to be involved in a God-centered local church dedicated to a "high view" of God, with preaching that expounds the truths of God's nature. A vibrant devotional life and involved congregational life cannot trouble-proof one's Christian walk, but each will greatly assist the believer in looking beyond this world to the realm where our Redeemer dwells.

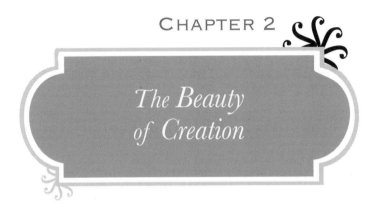

CHAPTER 2

The Beauty of Creation

*O*ne day, as a student, Jonathan Edwards took a walk in his father's pasture, meandering around stalks of grass, gazing at the sky. He later said of that stroll:

AND AS I WAS WALKING THERE, and looked up on the sky and clouds; there came into my mind, a sweet sense of the glorious majesty and grace of God, that I know not how to express. I seemed to see them both in a sweet conjunction: majesty and meekness joined together: it was a sweet and gentle, and holy majesty; and also a majestic meekness; an awful sweetness; a high, and great, and holy gentleness.

> After this my sense of divine things gradually increased, and became more and more lively, and had more of that inward sweetness. The appearance of everything was altered: there seemed to be, as it were, a calm, sweet cast, or appearance of divine glory, in almost everything. (*Works* 16, 793–4)

The walk was a special one, full of communion with the divine. It was by no means the only time in his life that Edwards tasted the beauty of God's created realm, however. A theologian with a deep love for nature, Edwards regularly meditated on the wisdom and beauty of God while walking, riding his horse, or working outside. So far from the stereotype of Edwards as a dry and dusty thinker, Edwards's love for nature reveals the deeply aesthetic side of the man.

This chapter examines Edwards's understanding of nature as a testimony to the beauty of God and the communication in visible form of His excellence. It examines several facets of his love for nature—that it was wisely designed, that it played a unique role in the display and reflection of the beauty of the Lord, and that it pictured certain spiritual realities, a study known as typology. In sum, we will see that Edwards loved nature for deeply biblical reasons and saw it as a living exhibition of the wisdom and beauty of God.

The Wise Design of Creation

From an early age, when most children are content simply to trample plants and animals, birds and trees, young Jonathan applied his mind to the science of nature and the workings of the world. When he was twenty, he published a brief treatise on the habits of spiders that won him international acclaim. Called the "Spider Letter," the document demonstrates Jonathan's powers of observation and reveals his early tendency to trace the hand of God in the world of nature:

> IN A VERY CALM SERENE DAY in the forementioned time of year, standing at some distance between the end of an house or some other opaque body, so as just to hide the disk of the sun and keep off his dazzling rays, and looking along close by the side of it, I have seen vast multitudes of little shining webs and glistening strings, brightly reflecting the sunbeams, and some of them of a great length, and at such a height that one would think that they were tacked to the vault of the heavens, and would be burnt like tow in the sun, making a very pleasing as well as surprising appearance. . . . But that which is most astonishing is that very often there appears at the end of these webs, spiders sailing in the air with them, doubtless with abundance of pleasure, though not with so much as I have beheld them and shewed them to others. And since I have seen these things I have been very conversant with spiders. (*Works* 16, 163–4)

Edwards showed an expert eye for the patterns and systems of the spider world. Behind this research and the curiosity that drove it was reverence for the natural order, a love nurtured by both the preaching of his father and his own exploration of nature. From his earliest days, Edwards saw what so many people miss in their modern rush of life, that the world contains great elegance and precise design. The young man saw these truths not simply in meadows and trees, but also in spiders, creatures that most people would rather run from than study. He knew, however, that God had created all things and that one could discover His beauty in even the strangest of places and the lowliest of creatures.

Finding God's imprint in the natural order was no theological rabbit trail, but was one of the most natural endeavors of mankind. God, it turned out, had placed humanity in His personal laboratory, with evidence of His presence flowing into all corners of the earth. Man's duty was not to ponder whether the divine scientist existed, but to study His creation in all of its intricate beauty.

Edwards showed a similar capacity for observation in a work entitled "Of the Rainbow." Where, he wondered out loud, does the rainbow come from? His answer included the following:

IT CANNOT BE THE CLOUD from whence this [rainbow] reflection is made, as was once thought, for we almost always see the ends of rainbows come down, even in amongst the trees, below the hills, and to the very ground, where we know there is no part of the cloud there but what descends in drops of rain. And [I] can convince any man by ocular demonstration in two minutes on a fair day that the reflection is from drops, by only taking a little water into my mouth, and standing between the sun and something that looks a little darkish, and spirting of it into the air so as to disperse all into fine drops; and there will appear as complete and plain a rainbow, with all the colors, as ever was seen in the heavens. And there will appear the same, if the sun is near enough to the horizon, upon fine drops of water dashed up by a stick from a puddle. (*Works* 6, 298)

Edwards did not only study the spider in his backyard, he analyzed the strange and beautiful phenomena of the world around him. Though he had an aesthetic appreciation for the rainbow, Edwards's belief in a Creator-God also drove him to try to find a rationale for the rainbow's magical appearance. His analysis shows both a keen mind and a voracious curiosity, each of which he used to trace the Lord's craftsmanship in the created realm.

The Natural World as a Realm of Beauty

On the same day that Edwards took his deeply moving walk in his father's field, he found that:

GOD'S EXCELLENCY, HIS WISDOM, his purity and love, seemed to appear in everything; in the sun, moon and stars; in the clouds, and blue sky; in the grass, flowers, trees; in the water, and all nature; which used greatly to fix my mind. I often used to sit and view the moon, for a long time; and so in the daytime, spent much time in viewing the clouds and sky, to behold the sweet glory of God in these things: in the meantime, singing forth with a low voice, my contemplations of the Creator and Redeemer. And scarce anything, among all the works of nature, was so sweet to me as thunder and lightning. Formerly, nothing had been so terrible to me. I used to be a person uncommonly terrified with thunder: and it used to strike me with terror, when I saw a thunderstorm rising. But now, on the contrary, it rejoiced me. I felt God at the first appearance of a thunderstorm. And used to take the opportunity at such times, to fix myself to view the clouds, and see the lightnings play, and hear the majestic and awful voice of God's thunder: which often times was exceeding entertaining, leading me to sweet contemplations of my great and glorious God. And while I viewed, used to spend my time, as it always seemed natural to me, to sing or chant forth my meditations; to speak my thoughts in soliloquies, and speak with a singing voice. (*Works* 16, 794)

Earlier, we observed that Edwards found abundant evidence of a wise design in creation. During his meaningful nature walk, he focused on the created order as the physical display of the personal beauty of God and His works. He contemplated his physical surroundings "to behold the sweet glory of God in these things." With his high view of the Lord and His beauty, Edwards believed that it was only natural for the Lord to create a world in which His "excellent perfections" could shine. Not content with mere self-appreciation of His own beauty, He set in motion a cycle of glory that began with Himself and continued to the creation, a realm that reflected His character for all to see.

Edwards developed this doctrine in *The Dissertation Concerning the End for Which God Created the World*. There, he argued that:

> THERE IS AN INFINITE FULLNESS of all possible good in God, a fullness of every perfection, of all excellency and beauty, and of infinite happiness. And as this fullness is capable of communication or emanation . . . so it seems a thing amiable and valuable in itself that it should be communicated or flow forth, that this infinite fountain of good should send forth abundant streams, that this infinite fountain of light should, diffusing its excellent fullness, pour forth light all around. . . . Thus it is fit, since there is an infinite fountain of light and knowledge, that this light should shine forth in beams of communicated knowledge and

understanding: and as there is an infinite fountain of holiness, moral excellence and beauty, so it should flow out in
communicated holiness. And that as there is an infinite
fullness of joy and happiness, so these should have an ema-
nation, and become a fountain flowing out in abundant
streams, as beams from the sun. (*Works* 8, 432–33)

As Edwards conceived it, the world was no product of chance.
Every atom and molecule is created, on the contrary, to
receive and display the beauty and glory of God. The Lord is
"an infinite fountain of holiness, moral excellence, and
beauty," and the earth is the basin into which His beauty is
poured. In Edwards's eyes, the earth drinks richly from this
fountain, for heaven "send[s] forth abundant streams" with
the same intensity and frequency "as beams from the sun."
Just as the sun continuously sends out its rays, the rays of the
Lord's splendor flow without interruption into the earth, the
catch-basin of God's glory.

God declared His absolute supremacy throughout Scripture, Edwards noted, providing abundant testimony to the
theologian's argument that nature existed to display and
reflect the beauty of the Lord. "It is manifest," the pastor
declared:

THAT THE SCRIPTURES SPEAK, on all occasions, as though
God made himself his end in all his works: and as though
the same Being, who is the first cause of all things, were the
supreme and last end of all things. Thus in Isaiah 44:6,

"Thus saith the Lord, the King of Israel, and his redeemer the Lord of hosts, I am the first, I also am the last, and besides me there is no God." Isaiah 48:12, "I am the first, and I am the last." Revelation 1:8, "I am Alpha and Omega, the beginning and the ending, saith the Lord, which is, and was, and which is to come, the Almighty." Revelation 1:11, "I am Alpha and Omega, the first and the last." Revelation 1:17, "I am the first and the last." Revelation 21:6, "And he said unto me, it is done, I am Alpha and Omega, the beginning and the end." Revelation 22:13, "I am Alpha and Omega, the beginning and the end, the first and the last."

Edwards then interpreted these lofty statements:

AND WHEN GOD is so often spoken of as the last as well as the first, and the end as well as the beginning, what is meant (or at least implied) is, that as he is the first efficient cause and fountain from whence all things originate, so he is the last final cause for which they are made; the final term to which they all tend in their ultimate issue. This seems to be the most natural import of these expressions; and is confirmed by other parallel passages, as Romans 11:36, "For of him and through him and to him are all things." Colossians 1:16, "For by him were all things created, that are in heaven, and that are in earth, visible and invisible, whether they be thrones or dominions, principalities

or powers, all things were created by him, and for him."
Hebrews 2:10, "For it became him, by whom are all things,
and for whom are all things." In Proverbs 16:4 'tis said
expressly, "The Lord hath made all things for himself."
(*Works* 8, 467)

These citations testify to the point Edwards made about the
purpose of creation. In the biblical mind, creation is not an
end in itself. It is a subordinate realm, a place made by the
Lord for His purposes, chief of which is His self-glorification.
When humanity praises nature for its beauty and fails to
acknowledge God's authorship, it commits serious blasphemy.
The world is beautiful in many respects, but in all of these
the glory of God is displayed like a towering neon sign planted
by the Almighty. In Edwards's theology, one cannot logically
identify a scene of beauty and leave it disconnected from the
character of its designer. Wherever one finds instances of
beauty, one sees a picture and reflection of the "Alpha and
Omega," the one who "made all things for himself."

It was from this foundation that the pastor understood all
the sweet scenes the natural order provided. In "Beauty of the
World," an early piece on nature by Edwards, he discussed
various aspects of the creation with an eye to the design—
and Designer—behind them:

[T]HERE IS A GREAT SUITABLENESS between the objects of
different senses, as between sounds, colors, and smells as
between the colors of the woods and flowers, and the smell,

and the singing of birds—which 'tis probable consist in a
certain proportion of the vibrations that are made in the
different organs. So there are innumerable other agree-
ablenesses of motions, figures, etc.: the gentle motions of
trees, of lily, etc., as it is agreeable to other things that represent calmness, gentleness and benevolence, etc. The fields
and woods seem to rejoice, and how joyful do the birds
seem to be in it. How much a resemblance is there of every
grace in the fields covered with plants and flowers, when
the sun shines serenely and undisturbedly upon them.
How a resemblance, I say, of every grace and beautiful disposition of mind; of an inferior towards a superior cause, pre-
server, benevolent benefactor, and a fountain of happiness.

The harmony and order of creation, reflected in things like
"the number of vibrations that are caused in the optic nerve"
and the "agreablenesses of motions" of trees and plants, testified in the eyes of Edwards to "a superior cause" and a
"benevolent benefactor." Such were easily observable glimpses
of natural beauty. Another type existed as well, as Edwards
saw it:

THE LATTER SORT ARE THOSE BEAUTIES that delight us
and we can't tell why. Thus we find ourselves pleased in
beholding the color of the violets, but we know not what
secret regularity or harmony it is that creates that pleasure
in our minds. These hidden beauties are commonly by far

the greatest, because the more complex a beauty is, the more hidden is it. In this latter sort consists principally the beauty of the world; and very much in light and colors. [The].mixture of all sorts of rays, which we call white, is a proportionate mixture that is harmonious (as Sir Isaac Newton has shewn) to each particular simple color and contains in it some harmony or other that is delightful. And each sort of rays play a distinct tune to the soul, besides those lovely mixtures that are found in nature—those beau-ties, how lovely, in the green of the face of the earth, in all manner of colors in flowers, the color of the skies, and lovely tinctures of the morning and evening. (*Works* 6, 305–6)

The world was bursting with beauty, whether plainly seen or hidden from view. All of it called to humanity, playing "a dis-tinct tune to the soul" as with the mixed light rays identified by Isaac Newton. Creation was not pragmatic in Edwards's view. It was a love song from the Creator to mankind. In a thousand fields of study, God had coded the music of His cre-ation. One hears the music of God testifying to the beauty of God not only through musical notes, but through genes, and chemicals, and all the mysterious workings of nature.

The Effects of the Fall on Creation

The beauty of creation, however, was not pure. Unlike its Creator, creation was both subservient and fallen. In his unfinished *History of the Work of Redemption*, Edwards covered the fall of mankind and its effects on the creation:

> THIS LOWER WORLD BEFORE the fall enjoyed noonday light, the light of knowledge of God, the light of his glory and the light of his favor. But when man fell all this light was at once extinguished and the world reduced back again to total darkness, a worse darkness than that which was in the beginning of the world that we read of in the Genesis 1:2, "And the earth was without form and void [and darkness was upon the face of the deep]." This was a darkness a thousandfold worse or remediless as that neither man nor angels could find out any way whereby this darkness might be scattered. This darkness appeared in its blackness, then, when Adam and his wife first saw that they were naked and sewed fig leaves, and when they heard the voice of the Lord God walking in the midst [of the garden] and hid themselves among the trees of the garden. And then when God first called them to an account and said to Adam, "What is this that thou hast done, hast thou [eaten of the tree]?"—then we may suppose that their hearts were filled with shame and terror. (*Works* 9, 133)

When Adam and Eve sinned against God by listening to the serpent and eating the forbidden fruit from the tree of the

Knowledge of Good and Evil, they brought devastation upon the creation (see Genesis 3). Edwards does not dwell for long on the physical effects of the fall, but he believed that sin had marred this "lower world." One could find great beauty on the earth but also great ugliness and corruption. This passage does not weaken the celebratory tone of earlier quotations, but it does show that the beauty of creation, unlike the beauty of the Creator, weakened after the fall.

The fall disconnected man from His Creator. But this did not mean in Edwards's mind that God had left humanity without testimony to Himself and the truth of His Word. Edwards argued strongly throughout his career for the legitimacy of a field of study called *typology*. Typology is the study of biblical entities that foreshadow a larger reality. Many scholars believe that King David, for example, is a "type" of Christ, a shadow of the more majestic King to come, the Lord Jesus. Most interpreters confine their typology to the Bible, but Edwards, with his belief that all corners of the creation testify in some way to the Creator, unearthed countless "natural types" in the created realm.

Edwards laid out his view of typology in one selection of a notebook devoted to finding examples from the created order that pointed to spiritual truths. The pastor believed that lesser created things pointed to greater created things, as he recorded in his notebook:

THERE ARE SOME TYPES of divine things, both in Scripture and also in the works of nature and constitution of the world, that are much more lively than others. Everything seems to aim that way; and in some things the image is very lively, in others less lively, in others the image but faint and the resemblance in but few particulars with many things wherein there is a dissimilitude. God has ordered things in this respect much as he has in the natural world. He hath made man the head and end of this lower creation; and there are innumerable creatures that have some image of what is in men, but in an infinite variety of degrees. Animals have much more of a resemblance of what is in men than plants, plants much more than things inanimate.

Edwards justified this view by an appeal to numerous scriptural texts:

THAT NATURAL THINGS were ordered for types of spiritual things seems evident by these texts: John 1:9, "This was the true Light, which lighteth every man that cometh into the world"; and John 15:1, "I am the true vine." Things are thus said to be true in Scripture, in contradistinction to what is typical. The type is only the representation or shadow of the thing, but the antitype is the very substance, and is the true thing. Thus heaven is said to be the true holy of holies, in opposition to the holy of holies in the tabernacle and temple. Hebrews 9:24, "For Christ is not entered into the holy places made with hands, which are figures of the true; but into heaven itself, now to appear in the presence of God for us." So the spiritual gospel tabernacle is said to be the true tabernacle, in opposition to the legal typical tabernacle which was literally a tabernacle. Hebrews 8:2, "A minister of the sanctuary, and of the true tabernacle, which the Lord pitched, and not man."

Though few Christians today would approach biblical interpretation in this way, Edwards's arguments deserve consideration. Edwards was not like most of us, who have the modern tendency to compartmentalize our lives and segment parts of it off from our relationship with God. Rather, Edwards's view of God was large and encompassed every aspect of creation. In His great design, God had given "natural things" as types of "spiritual things." "Everything," said Edwards, "seems to aim that way."

One need not agree with every nuance of his typology to learn an important lesson from Edwards, namely, that the human-centered view of the universe so common in our day prevents us from a richer, fuller vision of the world and natural order. Psalm 19:1 rings in our ears on this point: "The heavens declare the glory of God, and the sky above proclaims his handiwork." Edwards applied this verse by finding types of spiritual truths in creation. His notebook entries are creative and lively. Of roses, Edwards said this:

ROSES GROW UPON BRIERS, which is to signify that all temporal sweets are mixed with bitter. But what seems more especially to be meant by it, is that true happiness, the crown of glory, is to be come at in no other way than by bearing Christ's cross by a life of mortification, self–denial and labor, and bearing all things for Christ. The rose, the chief of all flowers, is the last thing that comes out. The briery prickly bush grows before, but the end and crown of all is the beautiful and fragrant rose. (*Works* 11, 52)

In the sea, Edwards discovered the wrath of God:

THE WAVES AND BILLOWS of the sea in a storm and the dire cataracts there are of rivers have a representation of the terrible wrath of God, and amazing misery of [them] that endure it. Misery is often compared to waters in the Scripture—a being overwhelmed in waters. God's wrath is compared to waves and billows (Psalms 88:7, Psalms 42:7). Job 27:20, "Terrors take hold as waters." Hosea 5:10, "I will pour out my wrath upon them like water." In Psalms 42:7, God's wrath is expressly compared to cataracts of water: "Deep calleth unto deep at the noise of thy waterspouts." And the same is represented in hail and stormy winds, black clouds and thunder, etc. (*Works* 11, 58)

In the silkworm, Edwards saw Christ:

THE SILKWORM IS A REMARKABLE type of Christ, which, when it dies, yields us that of which we make such glorious clothing. Christ became a worm for our sakes, and by his death finished that righteousness with which believers are clothed, and thereby procured that we should be clothed with robes of glory. See 2 Samuel 5:23–24 and Psalms 84:6; the valley of mulberry trees. (*Works* 11, 59)

In the serpent's cunning, Edwards glimpsed Satan's schemes:

IN THE MANNER IN WHICH BIRDS and squirrels that are charmed by serpents go into their mouths and are destroyed by them, is a lively representation of the manner in which sinners under the gospel are very often charmed and destroyed by the devil. The animal that is charmed by the serpent seems to be in great exercise and fear, screams and makes ado, but yet don't flee away. It comes nearer to the serpent, and then seems to have its distress increased and goes a little back again, but then comes still nearer than ever, and then appears as if greatly affrighted and runs or flies back again a little way, but yet don't flee quite away, and soon comes a little nearer and a little nearer with seeming fear and distress that drives 'em a little back between whiles, until at length they come so [near] that the serpent can lay hold of them: and so they become their prey. (*Works* 11, 71)

These lively explorations of the created order show how Edwards worked out his understanding of nature as a display of God's glory and wisdom. In Edwards's worldview, the Creator planted these figments of Himself and His truth in creation to stimulate the faith of mankind. Wherever one looked —roses, the sea, silkworms, or serpents—one found the hand and mind of God.

Edwards's God was simultaneously a designer, aesthete, and instructor. The natural order existed for the magnification, pleasure, and use of the one who created it. Even with the effects of the fall corrupting God's handiwork, the world still brimmed with beauty. Wherever one discovered intelligence, loveliness, or depictions of spiritual realities, one found prime evidence of God's design. Beauty was not a concept one could abstract from God, but was the very essence of God. Thus the realm God created displayed His beauty. Creation derived not from pragmatics, from a mere desire by the Creator to create. Creation existed because God desired to put His glory, His beauty, before a celestial audience.

In the pastor's eyes, creation sung the praises of God and exhibited the wisdom of God. One did not have to squint to see this truth; one had only to open one's eyes. If one stopped to look at the flight of spiders or the soft light of a rainbow, one saw a reflection of a figure still more beautiful than these; if one only stopped to listen, one could hear, however faintly, a distant song calling a fallen world to discover the beauty of the Lord.

Pursuing Beauty

Appreciating the Design of Creation

Christians need to take time to celebrate the intelligence of the creational order. Examples abound of God's wise design. In the natural workings of nature, we see God's wisdom (see Job 40:20–24, for example). In the subtleties of the human body, we see God's handiwork (Psalm 139:14). In the makeup of the cell, we see God's impossibly complex mind. We should follow the lead of Edwards when we make these discoveries and direct lavish praise to the Creator. His example reminds us that these findings are not coincidental—that an infinitely wise God dedicates His ingenuity to our natural world. We must overcome the influence of secularistic science and philosophy and free our hearts and voices to celebrate the intelligence of God. We need to clear space in our technologically saturated lives to recognize the wisdom of the Lord in the natural realm. Instead of lavishing praise on humanity, we should acknowledge with Edwards and the biblical authors that this place is filled with the beauty of God's wisdom (Psalm 136).

Marveling at the Beauty of Nature

*I*t is essential in today's busy world for Christians to find time to commune with God in nature. The created order bursts with the majesty of God and testifies to us of the reality of God (Jeremiah 10:12). We should, therefore, make time for nature. We could start by watching far less television and consuming far less web content and instead going on a walk in which we pray and think about the world before us. Theologian David Wells has spoken of the "thin selves" our modernized world creates, rendering us people so infatuated with "newness" and "progress" that we are unable to appreciate the beauty of life in its simplest forms. It is little surprise that so many who are spiritually thin have so little connection with nature. We would do well to return to nature, so to speak, and to enjoy it—singing praises, praying, laughing, contemplating small delights, communing with God in the realm created to testify of Him.

Looking for Spiritual Truth

*C*hristians do not need to adopt the whole of Edwards's model of typology to benefit from his radically God-centered worldview and its application to nature. We may not perceive silkworms as picturing salvation, but we can reorient our understanding of life and creation around the view that the world is the Lord's. Everything is His, and thus we should not view nature as a compartmentalized space where no spiritual truth may enter. "The heavens declare His handiwork," the Bible tells us, and we must hear and see this declaration (Psalm 19:1). Surely, there are natural "signs" or "types" of mercy and judgment—one thinks of a needed rain for the first and a raging storm for the second—and we need not feel unbiblical for thinking so.

Caring for Creation

*C*ertain sectors of evangelicalism have maligned Christians who express a desire to care for the world. Environmental concerns can surely get out of hand, but it seems logical when holding a God-centered view of creation to take action to preserve and care for it (see Leviticus 25:1–12 and Psalm 104). Christians who have such a view possess a unique opportunity for witness when they meet people who love the earth but have no faith in its Creator. Our care for the world, sensibly handled, can be both an act of worship and a means of evangelism.

Yearning for a Greater Realm

*E*ven as we care for the creation, we should remember that this world is not our home. The crucified King, Jesus Christ, is returning to this earth, and He will create a new heaven and a new earth when He comes (Revelation 21). In this realm the Father, Son, and Spirit will dwell with all who have trusted Jesus Christ as their Savior. This new heaven and earth will not contain poison and corruption as this earth does. It will be a perfect, happy, holy place. As we glimpse the effects of the fall in our daily lives, we can praise God that this world is not our home and thank Him that we will soon enter a place of beauty and love, where God dwells for all eternity with His people.

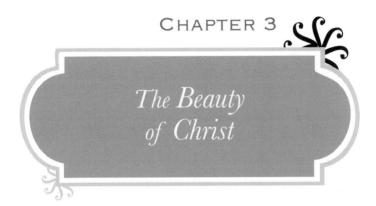

CHAPTER 3

The Beauty of Christ

The beauty of Christ often grips young believers. After years of sorrow and sin, the new believer finds hope and forgiveness through His atoning death and resurrection. Where things of the world once promised fulfillment, now the Christian finds satisfaction in spiritual pursuits. Over time, however, this delight can wane. Faith can grow dull. Christ can fade into the background. Where the believer once lived passionately for God, he now takes Him for granted. The difficulties of life seem huge, and Christ seems small, a far-off figure in the distance.

Jonathan Edwards knew this tendency of the human condition, this propensity of the heart to lose its passion for

Christ. He frequently preached sermons that exalted the Savior and that gave his church a breathtaking view of the second person of the Trinity. Edwards believed that Jesus was a vessel of beauty sent into the world to manifest the glory of God. He came to earth as the image of God, the exact likeness of His being (Colossians 1:15; Hebrews 1:3). Though He veiled His glory while on earth, Christ possessed beauty unlike any other living being. In his writings, Edwards lifted him up as the embodiment of beauty. He represents a manifestation of God's glory and forms part of the cycle of beauty that begins with the Lord, extends to creation, takes personal bodily form in Christ, is displayed corporately by the church, and culminates in heaven.

It is the purpose of this chapter to present several of Edwards's descriptions of the Savior's excellence. Here the reader will find some of the richest material Edwards ever produced. The pastor emphasized the beauty of Christ in a multitude of sermons throughout his career. Though all are worthy of study, a few stand out: "Christ the Light of the World," "Honey from the Rock," "Seeking after Christ," and the capstone of the genre, "The Excellency of Christ."

The Sweetness of Jesus Christ

We begin with "Christ the Light of the World," a sermon in which a young Edwards identified the special loveliness of the Lord:

THERE IS SCARCELY ANYTHING that is excellent, beautiful, pleasant, or profitable but what is used in the Scripture as an emblem of Christ. He is called a lion for his great power, victory, and glorious conquests; he is called a lamb for his great love, pity, and compassion: for that merciful, compassionate, condescending, lamblike disposition of his; for his humility, meekness, and great patience, and because he was slain like a lamb. He was brought as a lamb to the slaughter, so he opened not his mouth. He is called the bread of life and water of life, for the spiritual refreshment and nourishment he gives to the soul; he is called the true vine, because he communicates life to his members, and yields that comfort to the soul that refreshes it as the fruit of the vine doth the body; he is called life, for he is the life of the soul. He is called a rose and lily, and other such similitudes, because of his transcendent beauty and fragrancy. He is called the bright and morning star, and the sun of righteousness; and in our text, the light of the world, of which it is our business at present to speak. (*Works* 10, 535)

This section is noteworthy for the plethora of images Edwards uses to describe the unique beauty of the Son of God—"lion," "lamb," "bread and water of life," "true vine," "life," "rose and lily," "bright and morning star," "sun of righteousness," and "light of the world." This collection of images speaks to the young preacher's impressive grasp of biblical theology. Unlike some preachers today, who pay little attention to the development of a given idea in Scripture, Edwards frequently searched the whole canon to enrich his exegesis.

Creation revealed the beauty of God, as depicted in the last chapter, but Jesus Christ displayed the loveliness of the Godhead in an even more direct way. He was, after all, God in human flesh, and as such shone with a special light. As Edwards explains:

> GOD THE FATHER IS an infinite fountain of light, but Jesus Christ is the communication of this light. Some compare God the Father to the sun and Jesus Christ to the light that streams forth from him by which the world is enlightened. God the Father, in himself, was never seen: 'tis God the Son that has been the light that hath revealed him. God is an infinitely bright and glorious being, but Jesus Christ is that brightness of his glory by which he is revealed to us: "No man hath seen God at any time, but the only begotten Son, which is in the bosom of the Father, he hath declared him" (John 1:18). (*Works* 10, 535–36)

In light Edwards found an excellent analogy for Christ, for the mind could easily conceive of light as simultaneously pure, beautiful, and glorious. When the sun shone, it powerfully affected that which received its rays, warming cold bodies, banishing darkness. So it was with Christ, "that brightness" of the Father's glory.

Edwards described in vivid detail the ways in which Christ's light manifested glory in the hearts of sinners:

> BEFORE HE SHINES into men's souls, they are dead and dull in a deep sleep, are not diligent at their work, but lie still and sleep and do nothing respecting their souls. All their affections are dead, dull and lifeless; their understandings are darkened with the dark shades of spiritual night, and there is nothing but spiritual sleep and death in their souls.
>
> But when Christ arises upon them, then all things begin to revive, the will and affections begin to move, and they set about the work they have to do. They are now awakened out of their sleep: whereas they were still before, now they begin to be diligent and industrious; whereas they were silent before, now they begin to sing forth God's praises. Their graces now begin to be put into exercise, as flowers send forth a fragrancy when the sun shines upon them. (*Works* 10, 540)

Converting to Christ was no mere transaction in Edwards's mind. It signaled the awakening of one's "will and affections" for the Savior. Faith as Edwards conceived it involved a full-hearted embrace of Christ. The converted believer experienced a transformation of heart and mind, rising to spiritual life out of "spiritual sleep and death." As they learned to live for Christ, they sent "forth a fragrancy" that smelled of the Son. When Christ claimed a person, He made them anew, and made them to smell and look like Him.

The Satisfier of the Soul

In "Honey from the Rock," Edwards switched the metaphor from light to a rock, but continued the theme of Christ's all-sufficient and soul-satisfying work in the hearts of believers. As described in the book of Deuteronomy, Christ's "meanness," His lowliness, concealed a river of delights, just as the rock Moses struck burst with water in the parched desert (Exodus 17:6):

IT WAS A WONDERFUL WORK of God in the wilderness when he caused water to gush out of the rock, upon Moses' smiting of it with his rod, in such abundance as to supply all the congregation, and is spoken of as such; Deuteronomy 8:15, "Who led thee through that great and terrible wilderness, wherein were fiery serpents, and scorpions, and drought, where there was no water; who brought thee forth water out of the rock of flint." But this was but a little thing to this glorious work that is typified by it. It was a glorious work of God's power, as well as mercy, to provide such blessings for a lost world by Jesus Christ. It was wonderful that such blessings should be made to flow from this rock, whether we consider this similitude of a rock as denoting his outward meanness or his divine greatness. (*Works* 10, 137)

Edwards concluded the section with a summation of the qualities of Christ's beauty:

AND 'TIS WONDERFUL ALSO if we consider Christ's divine greatness, for this is also signified by this metaphor of a rock. As we have shown, it signifies his divine perfection and holiness, his omnipotence, his eternity, his immutability. Now, 'tis a wonderful work of God that such a glorious person should be made the head of influence and fountain of spiritual nourishment to lost mankind: that so great, so glorious a person should be given to us, to be to us a fountain of blessings to be enjoyed by us who are so mean and unworthy. (*Works* 10, 137–38)

In this discussion, Edwards interpreted the rock Moses struck in a Christological way, arguing that beneath Christ's exterior flowed an unending channel of God's love and beauty. The interpretation is imaginative and moving. Few of us, after all, have too large a view of God. Most of us have far too small a view of God and His goodness. Edwards shows us that Christ is nothing less than "a fountain of blessings" for His people. Moses had only a single chance to strike the rock; we have constant access to the stream of the blessings of Christ's person. Every Christian, whatever their circumstances, has equal and absolute access to Christ and all His glorious perfections.

Access to Divine Loveliness

Edwards continued this awesome theme in "Seeking After Christ." When a person seeks after the Son of God, he declared:

THE PERSON THAT THEY FIND is exceeding excellent and lovely. Before Christ is found, there is nothing that is truly lovely that is ever found or seen. Those things that they had been conversant with before and had set their hearts upon, had no true excellency. They only deceived 'em with a false, empty show. But now they have found Christ, they have found one that is excellent indeed. They see in him a real and substantial excellency.

It was not always so. Before the sinner comes to Christ, they find Him a subject of "fear and terror":

BEFORE THAT, while they were under trouble, they had before them only those things that were objects of fear and terror, such as their own guilt, the wickedness of their hearts, and the wrath of God, and death and hell, but noth-ing pleasant or lovely. But [when] they came to find Christ, what was terrible in those objects disappears, and they found a glorious object and far surpassing all things that ever they saw, one of excellent majesty and of perfect purity and brightness, purer than the light of the sun, infinitely farther from all deformity or defilement than the highest heavens themselves; and this conjoined with the sweetest grace, one that clothes himself with mildness and meekness and love. How refreshing and rejoicing must this be after they have nothing before their eyes but their sins staring them in the face, appearing with a frightful countenance, and God's terrible anger, and frightful devils, and death's pale and ghastly countenance, and the devouring flames of hell. How exceeding refreshing must it be to find so lovely an object after they have so long had nothing but such objects before 'em. (*Works* 22, 289)

This section offers a simple but striking summation of the differences between the hope of the unbeliever and the believer. Try as they might, the unbeliever cannot access any lasting, meaningful kind of hope. All that appears hopeful is in the end unfulfilling. "Fear and terror," "guilt," "the wrath of God," and "death and hell" plague them all their days. Those who appear happiest often end up being the least happy and most fearful people we know. Those who appear most confident and precise in their thinking often live with ethical turmoil and intellectual confusion. The absence of Christ leaves a hole that nothing can fill.

When Christ claims a person, however, everything changes. The lost soul, tormented with terrible thoughts and a guilty conscience, discovers "a glorious object," a being "of excellent majesty and of perfect purity and brightness," whose love brings "the sweetest grace." There is an element in these words of *eros*, romantic attraction, that few today would understand but was a staple of Edwards's descriptions of the love between God and His people. In his view, it was entirely proper that the church, gazing on the beatific Son of God, feel the deepest passion for Him, a deep affection that transcended physicality and represented the purest form of covenantal love.

The Comfort of the Savior

Edwards developed a different image of the Savior in "Christ the Spiritual Sun." He discussed first how the Son comforted believers with His presence:

THE HEARTS OF TRUE BELIEVERS are greatly comforted and refreshed with the beams of this. The day that this Sun brings on, when it arises, is a pleasant day to them. As the light of the sun is sweet to the bodily eye, so, and much more, is the light of the spiritual Sun sweet to the spiritual eye of the believer. It is a pleasant thing for the eye to behold the sun, but much more pleasant to a believer to behold Jesus Christ that is fairer than the sons of men [Psalms 45:2]. It is refreshing to see the light of the sun down in the east to a man that has been lost and long wandering in the night, in a wilderness, groping in darkness, not knowing whither he went; but much more refreshing and sweet to behold the dawning light of the Sun of righteousness.

Edwards's love for nature is evident in his celebration of Christ:

HOW DOES THE FACE of the Earth seem to rejoice when the sun comes to shine pleasantly upon it in the spring. The pastures are clothed with green grass and many pleas-ant flowers that open their bosom to receive the subeams. How are the trees as it were clothed with garments of rejoicing, with green leaves and beautiful and fragrant blossoms, as though they sang and shouted for joy at the influences of the sun. Psalms 65:13, "The pastures are clothed with flocks; the valleys also."

This is a lively image of that sweet spiritual comfort, joy and excellent refreshment that the souls of believers have under the beams of the Sun of righteousness. (*Works* 22, 55–56)

Christ not only nourished the believer, but restored their soul in the midst of pain and suffering brought on by sin and a fallen world:

THE BEAMS OF THIS spiritual Sun don't only refresh but restore the souls of believers. Thus it is said that the Sun of righteousness [shall arise] with healing [in his wings]. These beams heal the souls of believers. As we often see that when the trees or plants of the earth are wounded, the beams of the sun will heal the wound and by degrees restore the plant, so the sweet beams of the Sun of righteousness heal the wounds of believers' souls. When they have been wounded by sin and have labored under the pain of wounds of conscience, the rays of this Sun heal the wounds of conscience. When they have been wounded by temptation and made to fall to their hurt, those benign beams, when they come to shine on the wounded soul, restore and heal the hurt that has been received.

The pastor powerfully described the tender ministry of Christ to His people:

THE SICK SOUL BY THESE BEAMS is restored, as plants that have grown in shady and cold places appear sickly and languishing, if the shade be removed and the sunbeams come to shine down upon them, will revive and flourish; or as the clear shining of the sun after the rain.

The beams of this Sun heal of the mortal poison of the fiery serpent, as the children of Israel were healed by looking on the brazen serpent in the wilderness. Yea, these beams don't only restore from wounds but from death; they don't only give light but life. The soul of a convert is raised from the dead by the shining of the beams of this Sun, as we see the rays of the sun in the spring revives the grass and herbs as it were from the dead and causes a resurrection of them from the dust, making 'em to spring out of the ground with new life. The beams of the Sun of righteousness, when it rises in the morning of the last day, will revive not only the souls but the bodies of the saints, will cause at once an universal resurrection of them; as we see in the morning when the sun returns, it causes all animals to rise out of a state of darkness and sleep, which is the image of darkness. (*Works* 22, 56–7)

Edwards's depiction of Christ as a sun made clear that His emanations warmed the soul just as the physical sun warmed the body. The believer, beset by personal sin, would find it constantly "refreshing and sweet to behold the dawning light of the Sun of righteousness." Christ infused the heart of the Christian with a radiant warmth, a sense of absolute love that brought fresh hope to the heart and fresh confidence to the mind.

Christ also took on the work of restoring the heart. Edwards preached that as "the beams of the sun will heal the wound and by degrees restore the plant, so the sweet beams of the Sun of righteousness heal the wounds of believers' souls." The shining beauty of the Son gives life to hurting believers. Constantly wounded, either by oneself or by others, the Christian finds restoration and hope in their personal connection to the "Sun of righteousness." When believers trap themselves in a pattern of sin, Christ imparts fresh forgiveness to them; when sinned against, Christ reassures the believer, reminding them of their acceptance in the beloved.

The Majesty of the Son

Edwards's preaching on Christ reached its apex in the classic sermon "The Excellency of Christ." Based on Revelation 5:5–6, the passage in which Christ is depicted as both a lion and a lamb, the sermon presented Edwards's insights on the "admirable conjunction of diverse excellencies in Jesus Christ." The first of these conjunctions was the simultaneous condescension and highness of Jesus Christ, the one both "infinitely great" and "low and mean," as Edwards put it. First, the pastor covered His "infinite highness":

THERE DO MEET IN JESUS CHRIST, infinite highness, and infinite condescension. Christ, as he is God, is infinitely great and high above all. He is higher than the kings of the earth; for he is King of Kings, and Lord of Lords. He is higher than the heavens, and higher than the highest angels of heaven. So great is he, that all men, all kings and princes, are as worms of the dust before him, all nations are as the drop of the bucket, and the light dust of the balance; yea, and angels themselves are as nothing before him. He is so high, that he is infinitely above any need of us; above our reach, that we cannot be profitable to him, and above our conceptions, that we cannot comprehend him. Proverbs 30:4, "What is his name, and what is his Son's name, if thou canst tell?" Our understandings, if we stretch them never so far, can't reach up to his divine glory. Job 11:8, "It is high as heaven, what canst thou do?" Christ is the Creator, and great possessor of heaven and earth: he is sovereign lord of all: he rules over the whole universe, and doth whatsoever pleaseth him: his knowledge is without bound: his wisdom is perfect, and what none can circumvent: his power is infinite, and none can resist him: his riches are immense and inexhaustible: his majesty is infinitely awful.

He then discussed the "infinite condescension" of the Savior:

AND YET HE IS ONE of infinite condescension. None are so low, or inferior, but Christ's condescension is sufficient to take a gracious notice of them. He condescends not only to the angels, humbling himself to behold the things that are done in heaven, but he also condescends to such poor creatures as men; and that not only so as to take notice of princes and great men, but of those that are of meanest rank and degree, "the poor of the world" (James 2:5). Such as are commonly despised by their fellow creatures, Christ don't despise. 1 Corinthians 1:28, "Base things of the world, and things that are despised, hath God chosen." Christ condescends to take notice of beggars (Luke 16:22) and of servants, and people of the most despised nations: in Christ Jesus is neither "Barbarian, Scythian, bond, nor free" (Colossians 3:11). He that is thus high, condescends to take a gracious notice of little children. Matthew 19:14, "Suffer little children to come unto me." Yea, which is much more, his condescension is sufficient to take a gracious notice of the most unworthy, sinful creatures, those that have no good deservings, and those that have infinite ill deservings. (*Works* 19, 565–66)

Next Edwards considered the "infinite justice" and "infinite grace" of Christ:

THERE MEET IN JESUS CHRIST, infinite justice, and infinite grace. As Christ is a divine person he is infinitely holy and just, infinitely hating sin, and disposed to execute condign punishment for sin. He is the Judge of the world, and the infinitely just judge of it, and will not at all acquit the wicked, or by any means clear the guilty.

And yet he is one that is infinitely gracious and mer–
ciful. Though his justice be so strict with respect to all sin,
and every breach of the law, yet he has grace sufficient for
every sinner, and even the chief of sinners. And it is not
only sufficient for the most unworthy to show them mercy,
and bestow some good upon them, but to bestow the
greatest good; yea, 'tis sufficient to bestow all good upon
them, and to do all things for them. There is no benefit or
blessing that they can receive so great, but the grace of
Christ is sufficient to bestow it on the greatest sinner that
ever lived. And not only so, but so great is his grace, that
nothing is too much as the means of this good: 'tis suffi–
cient not only to do great things, but also to suffer in order
to it; and not only to suffer, but to suffer most extremely,
even unto death, the most terrible of natural evils; and not
only death, but the most ignominious and tormenting, and
every way the most terrible death that men could inflict;
yea, and greater sufferings than men could inflict, who
could only torment the body, but also those sufferings in
his soul, that were the more immediate fruits of the wrath
of God against the sins of those he undertakes for. (*Works* 19,
567)

Few written documents so capture the beauty of Christ and
His work as "The Excellency of Christ." The sermon in its

entirety deserves careful reading and meditation by every Christian. It is a masterpiece. Here, Edwards offered his people a picture of Jesus Christ that elegantly balanced the traits of majesty and humility, grace and justice. Never before had such a figure existed. Never had one person sustained such paradox, such tension, in their inner being, and carried both the majesty of heaven and the meekness of earth in their flesh. As majestic and "terrible" as one could be, Jesus was and is; as humble and kind as one could be, Jesus was and is.

These traits were not merely admirable. They were foundational for the crucifixion Christ faced for the salvation of the lost. Edwards next discussed the beauty Christ displayed in His atoning death, focusing first on how He showed His love for His Father:

> HE NEVER IN ANY ACT gave so great a manifestation of love to God, and yet never so manifested his love to those that were enemies to God, as in that act. Christ never did anything whereby his love to the Father was so eminently manifested, as in his laying down his life, under such inexpressible sufferings, in obedience to his command, and for the vindication of the honor of his authority and majesty; nor did ever any mere creature give such a testimony of love to God as that was: and yet this was the greatest expression of all, of his love to sinful men, that were enemies to God. Romans 5:10, "While we were enemies, we were reconciled to God, by the death of his Son." The great-

ness of Christ's love to such, appears in nothing so much, as in its being dying love. That blood of Christ that was sweat out, and fell in great drops to the ground, in his agony, was shed from love to God's enemies, and his own. That shame and spitting, that torment of body, and that exceeding sorrow, even unto death, that he endured in his soul, was what he underwent from love to rebels against God, to save them from hell, and to purchase for them eternal glory. Never did Christ so eminently show his regard to God's honor, as in offering up himself a victim to revenging justice, to vindicate God's honor: and yet in this above all, he manifested his love to them that dishonored God, so as to bring such guilt on themselves, that nothing less than his blood could atone for it.

Next Edwards considered how Christ's atonement satisfied divine justice:

CHRIST NEVER SO EMINENTLY appeared for divine justice, and yet never suffered so much from divine justice, as when he offered up himself a sacrifice for our sins. In Christ's great sufferings, did his infinite regard to the honor of God's justice distinguishingly appear; for it was from regard to that, that he thus humbled himself: and yet in these sufferings, Christ was the mark of the vindictive expressions of that very justice of God. Revenging justice then spent all its force upon him, on account of our guilt that was laid upon him; he was not spared at all; but God spent the arrows of his vengeance upon him, which made him sweat blood, and cry out upon the cross, and probably rent his vitals, broke his heart, the fountain of blood, or some other internal blood vessels, and by the violent fermentation turned his blood to water: for the blood and water that issued out of his side, when pierced by the spear, seems to have been extravasated blood; and so there might be a kind of literal fulfillment of that, in Psalms 22:14, "I am poured out like water, and all my bones are out of joint: my heart is like wax, it is melted in the midst of my bowels." And this was the way and means by which Christ stood up for the honor of God's justice, viz. by thus suffering its terrible executions. For when he had undertaken for sinners, and had substituted himself in their room, divine justice could have its due honor, no other way than by his suffering its revenges. (*Works* 19, 577–78)

The one who bore "the arrows" of God's justice was Himself shot into the world by God to pierce the heart of sin and death. Each fiber of His being was perfectly tuned for the cross so that the "enemies of God" might taste life and the "justice of God" find its eternal vindication. This latter burden formed Christ's ultimate concern. Christ gave His life for "rebels," but He cared above all for "God's honor" and reputation. For Edwards, the cross, as with all things, found its highest significance in relation to its glorification of God. Jesus loved the lost, and suffered "terrible executions" of wrath to save them from hell. But the character and reputation of God was Christ's highest concern in bearing the Father's "vengeance" for sin. In the world made to display the beauty of God, the Son's obedience to the Father elevated Him above all, rendering Him worthy of eternal adoration and praise.

Proclaiming Christ's Beauty

Jonathan Edwards devoted a large part of his pastoral career to expounding the magnificent beauty of the Son of God. He used every fitting analogy he could find to unfurl the glory of Christ, referencing light, rocks, the sun, lions and lambs, and more. He strove to bring his congregation and all who would read his works into the realm where the clouds of this world lift and the glory of the risen Lord is all that is visible. The colonial theologian showed Christ to be a Savior who takes our breath away at the sight of His beauty.

Pursuing Beauty

Cultivating a Large View of Christ

*I*n the same way that we need a large view of the Father, we need a large view of the Son, the Savior of the world. In some churches, Christ is reduced to a set of facts one believes, a mystical friend one spends time with, or a spiritual service repairman one calls when in need. In the Bible, Christ is the majestic Son of God who reigns over the universe He created. He is lordly, awesome, and terrible, even as He is kind, gentle, and loving. It is of first importance with Edwards that we get Christ's person right. The Scripture depicts Christ as the beginning and end of all things, the central character in the plotline of Scripture and of human history, and we must think of Him as such. Our first order of application, then, is simply to think about Christ in biblical categories.

Thinking Less About Ourselves

*T*he world encourages us to focus an inordinate amount of attention on ourselves and our concerns. We are coaxed by countless voices to "stay true to ourselves," to "focus on me for a while," to "not let anyone tell me what to do." The study of Edwards's material on Christ hits the mute button on the world and allows us to break free from our self-interests and revel in the glory of Christ. It shows us that our central need is not to become psychologically satisfied, but to treasure Jesus Christ above all things by bowing in repentance and worship before Him (Hebrews 3:1–6). Each day that we live is an opportunity not to glorify our sinful selves, but to glorify the one who bled and died for our salvation, our liberation from Satan's shackles. Let us clear space in our hearts for adoration not of ourselves, but of Christ. Life is not about us. It is about Jesus Christ and a fixed, unrelenting, soul-satisfying pursuit of Him.

Stoking Our Love for Christ

*I*f we would follow Christ and honor Him by obedient lives, we must learn to love Him. We must cultivate affection for Christ through study of the Bible and prayer that celebrates Christ's person and work. We need to see the Bible as a book that testifies to Christ in both direct and indirect ways (Matthew 5:17–20; Luke 24:27, 44). We need to bring before our ears and eyes teaching that exalts Christ, turning off and tuning out chatterbox media that do nothing to energize our love for Him. We need to praise the Father in our prayers for Jesus Christ and all His perfections. We can use material like that left for us by Edwards, working our way through a sermon like "The Excellency of Christ" on our lunch break or our evening downtime. The challenge is simply this: to think much about Christ. We need to stoke our hearts to think about Him not just on Sunday morning, but all throughout the week, such that we are Christ-saturated, brimming with affection and love for Him (see Colossians 3:1–10).

Of primary importance in shaping such a heart is a local church that centers itself not around numbers, programs, or vague spirituality, but a living, reigning Lord who leads the church in its life and mission. When a church is truly Christ-centered, preaching Christ as the center not only of Scripture but of all of life, its members will not be able to resist catching a Christocentric vision for life.

Evangelizing With an Eye to the King's Return

*T*he reality that Christ died as a lamb but will return as a king must motivate us to share the gospel with all that we can. When Christ returns, He will not come again in peace and gentleness, but as a triumphant warrior-king (see Revelation 1 and following). This return is imminent, meaning it could happen at any moment (1 Thessalonians 4:13–17). Until Christ comes, He has given His people the mission of calling people to repentance and faith in Him—a mission that the Spirit aids and that promises to advance with force if Christ's people will only take it up (Matthew 28:16–20; Acts 1:8). Methods and styles of evangelism will vary, but all Christians need to catch a vision for sharing the love of God with as many as they can and warning fellow sinners about the judgment of God. In our churches, workplaces, gyms, and neighborhoods, we must introduce people to the surpassing mercy of the lamb so that they do not one day taste the judgment of the lion.

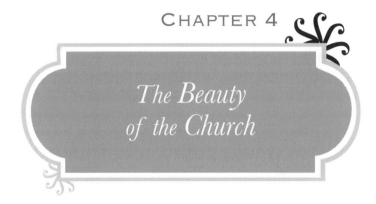

CHAPTER 4

The Beauty of the Church

For many Christians, the church would not normally be considered an object of beauty. In common evangelical parlance, the church is a building, a collection of bricks and mortar that houses the activity of Christians. Little wonder that so many people profess so little love for the church. When coupled with a bad experience or two, the church can feel impersonal, cold, and lifeless.

It shouldn't be this way. In one section of his "Notes on Scripture," Jonathan Edwards sketched a simple portrait of the *ecclesia* that drives to the heart of the church's identity. Edwards suggested:

> THAT GOD'S CHURCH, that in Scripture is represented as
> Christ's house or temple, and as his raiment and ornament,
> and as a golden candlestick, etc., is wholly constituted of
> those saints that are his jewels, that are the spoils of his
> enemies, that were once his enemies' possession, but that
> he has redeemed out of their hands. (*Works* 15, 337)

The church, Edwards noted, is the people of God, "those
saints that are his jewels," the diverse collection of believers
whom Christ rescued from "his enemies' possession." The
"ornament" of the Savior, His prized belonging, the church is
an entity unlike any other on the earth. Transcending organization or institution, the church is the "mystical body" of Jesus
Christ, according to other writings of Edwards, the living manifestation of the Lord in this realm that provides a picture of
the Savior for a world who has lost sight of Him.

With his capacious imagination, strong grasp of biblical
theology, and zeal for God, Edwards sketched a vision of the
church in his collected writings that promises to transform
our understanding of it. The church had both a holy identity
as the people of God and a profound role in the Edwardsean
cycle of beauty. The church, as with all the created order,
existed to reflect the holiness and goodness of God in a world
cursed by sin. It represented the lasting physical manifestation of God on earth, an outpost exhibiting the beauty of the
Lord in a darkened world.

In this chapter, we look at Edwards's understanding of the
role humanity plays in the scheme of God's cosmic plan. We

then examine two sources of Edwards's doctrine of the church: first, his "Notes on Scripture," and second, "The History of the Work of Redemption." The first text reveals Edwards's understanding of the nature of the church, while the second shows how Edwards saw the church fitting into the great story of the ages. Taken together, these texts reveal the character and purpose of the people of God, those whom Christ died to make His own for the glory of the Father.

The Church as a "Glorious Society"

As explored in the first chapter, Edwards believed that God was the preeminent one, the being for whom all things existed and in whom true beauty was found. Living in a realm that teemed with God's glory, mankind found its calling in joining with God in the work of His self-glorification. Edwards dictated this vision for human life in his *Dissertation Concerning the End for Which God Created the World.* In the section below, Edwards discusses how God created a "glorious society" to consciously display His own perfections:

> IT SEEMS TO BE A THING in itself fit and desirable, that the glorious perfections of God should be known, and the operations and expressions of them seen by other beings besides himself. If it be fit that God's power and wisdom, etc., should be exercised and expressed in some effects, and not lie eternally dormant, then it seems proper that these

exercises should appear, and not be totally hidden and unknown. . . . As God's perfections are things in themselves excellent, so the expression of them in their proper acts and fruits is excellent, and the knowledge of these excellent perfections, and of these glorious expressions of them, is an excellent thing, the existence of which is in itself valuable and desirable. 'Tis a thing infinitely good in itself that God's glory should be known by a glorious society of created beings. (*Works* 8, 430–2)

As Edwards makes clear, God desired that His beauty transcend passive representation, as rocks, trees, and oceans allow. He wanted His perfections to "be known" and considered according to self-conscious "knowledge." Here humanity found its reason for existence. The purpose of human life in Edwardsean thought is to know with the fullness of one's mind and senses the "excellent perfections" of God.

Thus, the race of mankind was created for this lofty end. As noted in chapter two, Edwards also asserted that God designed the world to satisfy the desires of the human beings He had formed for communion and love. The fall of Adam and Eve, however, resulted in the loss of this bounty. Though everyone in some sense would taste the goodness of God through life on earth, only those whom God called to be His children would join the "glorious society" dedicated to the adoration of the Almighty. Edwards identified this society as the church, which included the children of God of every age.

In every generation, it was the church's privilege to taste the Lord's goodness and love; in all seasons, it was the church's mission to celebrate and magnify this goodness in a foreign and hostile world.

The Church as an "Imperfect Embryo"

As mentioned at the beginning of the chapter, Edwards defined the church as the people of God in his "Notes on Scripture," an unpublished collection of reflections written over the course of the expositor's life. A different type of source than Edwards's polished sermons or refined theological treatises, the notes allow us to peer over Edwards's shoulder as he recorded insights in his study. Early in the notes Edwards mused:

> 47. JOHN 2:21. "But he spake of the temple of his body." And it seems to me likely that he should speak of his body in two senses: in one sense of the church, which is called his body, and is also called the temple of God, of which the temple of Jerusalem was a type. The temple of Jerusalem may signify the Jewish church, which Christ put an end to by his coming, and in three ages after erected his spiritual temple, the Christian church. (*Works* 15, 63)

Using the Old Testament, Edwards described how the Lord shaped His church into His temple:

1 KINGS 6:7. "And the house, when it was in building, was built of stone made ready before it was brought thither; so that there was neither hammer, nor ax, nor any tool of iron heard in the house, while it was in building." This temple represents the church of God, who are called God's temple, a spiritual house, Jesus Christ being chief cornerstone, and all the saints as so many stones. Particularly by Solomon's temple is meant the church triumphant, as by the tabernacle the church militant; by the exact fitting, squaring, and smoothing of those stones before they were brought thither, represents the perfection of the saints in glory. Heaven is not a place to prepare them; they are all prepared before they come there. They come perfectly sinless and holy into heaven. The world is the place where God hews them, and squares them by his prophets and ministers (1 Kings 5:6), by the reproofs and warnings of his word, which God compares to a hammer, by persecutions and afflictions. There shall be no noise of these tools heard in heaven, but all these lively stones of this spiritual and glorious building are exactly fitted, framed, and polished before they come there. (*Works* 15, 64)

Because Edwards so closely connected the Old and New Testaments, he was able to draw stunning comparisons between scriptural institutions and ideas. In this section, Edwards argued that the Lord fitted His church for heaven with the same care and precision that the Israelite craftsmen used to construct the great temple of the Lord. Here Edwards noted that God "hews" and "squares" His people, rendering them beautiful and holy in His sight. The divine craftsman employs biblical "reproofs and warnings" and temporal "persecutions and afflictions" to accomplish this end. Though Christians may at times feel downcast and beaten by their sufferings, Edwards's words remind the church that the sovereign Lord sends trials to beautify His people and leave them "fitted, framed, and polished" for the life to come where "no noise of these tools" will sound.

The Lord's blueprint for the church was Christ. As He fitted the church for heaven, the Lord conformed His people to the express image of the Son. Edwards explored this matter in a note on conformity:

> EPHESIANS 4:13. "Till we all come in the unity of the faith, and of the knowledge of the Son of God, to the measure of the stature of the fullness of Christ." That is, till we all come to agree in the same faith, which is fully conformed to Christ, and therein are come to his rule and measure; and in faith, and perhaps in other graces, the body of Christ becomes complete, being completely conformed to Christ. The church [is] the completeness of Christ, "the fullness of him that filleth all in all" [Ephesians 1:23]. But this body is not complete, and but an imperfect embryo, till it is perfectly

conformed to his mind in faith and to his image in other
graces. Christ and his church, as here, so elsewhere, being
as body and soul, are called one man. 'Tis as if he had said,
"Till Christ's body is complete in stature." The church, the
body of Christ, is called a man (Ephesians 2:15). (*Works* 15, 65)

Though an "imperfect embryo" and an inconsistent student
in the school of conformity, the church as Edwards conceived
it enjoyed a relationship with Christ so close that the two "are
called one man." The church was not simply an organization,
a like-minded group with leaders and helpers. The church was
the very body of Christ, the enfleshment of His being on the
earth. It enjoyed communion with Christ, its "soul," and
underwent spiritual transformation as the soul melded with
the body.

The Church as "Christ's Mother"

Edwards dwelt further on the spiritual union shared
between Christ and the church in his notes, describing in
intense, biblically saturated language the marriage between
them:

THE OLD TESTAMENT CHURCH was as Christ's mother, but
the New Testament church is his wife, whom he is joined to,
and whom he treats with far greater endearment and intimacy. He forsook his mother also in this respect, viz. as he
made a sacrifice of that flesh and blood, and laid down that

> mortal life which he had from his mother, the Virgin Mary.
> "That which [is] born of the flesh is flesh," though he did
> not derive flesh from his mother in the sense in which it is
> spoken of, John 3:6, viz. corrupt sinful nature, and therefore
> did not forsake his mother for the church in the same sense
> wherein the church is advised to forsake her father's house
> for Christ's sake, viz. to forsake sin and lusts derived from
> parents, by crucifying the flesh with the affections and lusts.
> Yet Christ derived flesh from his mother, viz. the animal
> nature and human nature, with that corruption that is the
> fruit of sin, viz. with frailty and mortality. This Christ for-
> sook, and yielded to be crucified for the sake of the church.
> (*Works* 15, 182)

The doctrine of the church developed here is quite unique.
Old Testament followers of God represent "Christ's mother,"
while New Testament believers are "his wife." The passage
emphasizes the "far greater endearment and intimacy" Christ
held for His wife. Christ "derived flesh" from the "human
nature" He assumed in His incarnation, which made possible
His "sacrifice" of "flesh and blood" given "for the sake of the
church" of all eras. Edwards shows a creative streak even as
he articulates a commonly held understanding of the atonement. Christ could not take an impure "wife"; He had to have
a pure bride, spotless and holy, and yet only He could provide
this purity for a sinful people. At the heart of the spiritual
unity between Christ and the church, then, is the cross which

made possible this unity and which cleansed the bride of every spot and blemish she bore.

Christ's gift to His bride extended beyond His sacrificial cleansing. In another note, Edwards discussed how, after saving His people, Christ "filled" them and satisfied their souls with His love, and was in turn satisfied by them. Referring to Ephesians 1:22–23, he wrote:

[H]ERE THE APOSTLE TEACHES that Christ, who fills all things, all elect creatures in heaven and earth, himself is filled by the church. He, who supplies angels and men with all that good in which they are perfect and happy, receives the church as that in which he himself is happy. He, from whom and in whom all angels and saints are adorned and made perfect in beauty, himself receives the church as his glorious and beautiful ornament, as the virtuous wife is a crown to her husband. The church is the garment of Christ, and was typified by that coat of his that was without seam [John 19:23], [which] signified the union of the various members of the church, and was typified by those garments of the high priest that were made "for glory and for beauty" (Exodus 28:2), as seems evident by the Psalms 133:2, and by the precious stones of his breastplate in a particular manner, on which were engraven the names of the children of Israel.

Edwards proved his point by reference to several Scriptures:

> ISAIAH 62:3, "Thou shalt also be a crown of glory in the
> hand of the Lord, and a royal diadem in the hand of thy
> God," i.e. in the possession of God. So Zechariah 9:16–17,
> "And the Lord their God shall save them in that day as the
> flock of his people, for they shall be as the stones of a
> crown, lifted up as an ensign upon his land." As 'tis from
> and in Christ that all are supplied with joy and happiness,
> so Christ receives the church as that in which he has
> exceeding and satisfying delight and joy. Isaiah 62:5, "As the
> bridegroom rejoiceth over the bride, so shall thy God
> rejoice over thee." This seems to be the good that Christ
> sought in the creation of the world, who is the beginning
> of the creation of God, when all things were created by him
> and for him, viz. that he might obtain a spouse that he
> might give himself to and give himself for, on whom he
> might pour forth his love, and in whom his soul might
> eternally be delighted. Till he had attained this, he was
> pleased not to look on himself as complete, but as wanting
> something, as Adam was not complete till he had obtained
> his Eve (Genesis 2:20). (*Works* 15, 185–86)

The passage covers several themes, not least among them the
matter of Christ's filling His bride. To be filled means that "ye

might have your souls satisfied with a participation of God's own good, his beauty and joy." The satisfaction of the Christian involved a constant sampling of God's goodness, a "participation" in the glory of His being. The Christian finds "fullness" of happiness and joy not from the world or anything in the world, but only in God. As believers seek the Lord, He fills them not simply with what is good but with His goodness, His beauty, His joy. The church, constantly "supplied with joy and happiness," is called to drink deeply of God and His goodness.

The Church as a "Multitude of Drops"

In turn, Edwards noted that "Christ, who fills all things, all elect creatures in heaven and earth, himself is filled by the church." Having made the church beautiful by His love, Jesus finds satisfaction in its beauty. Edwards did not believe that Christ needed the church to be happy, but instead thought that the church magnified Christ's existing happiness and self-satisfaction. The relationship of Christ and the church is a reciprocal one, then, with each party receiving joy in an unending cycle.

Having traced the way in which Christ nurtures and satisfies His people, Edwards went on to explore the beauty of both the individual believer and the church. Using the metaphor of a rainbow, Edwards discussed the role of each in the economy of divine beauty:

THE MULTITUDE OF DROPS, from which the light of the sun is so beautifully reflected, signify the same with the multitude of the drops of dew, that reflect the light of the sun in a morning, spoken of, Psalms 110:3. . . . They are all God's jewels; and as they are all in heaven, each one by its reflection is a little star, and so do more fitly represent the saints than the drops of dew. These drops are all from heaven, as the saints are born from above; they are all from the dissolving cloud. So the saints are the children of Christ; they receive their new nature from him, and by his death they are from the womb of the cloud, the church. So Jerusalem, which is above, is "the mother of us all" [Galatians 4:26]. The saints are born of the church that is in travail with them, enduring great labors, and sufferings, and cruel persecutions; so these jewels of God are out of the dissolving cloud. These drops receive and reflect the light of the sun just breaking forth, and shining out of the cloud that had been till now darkened, and hid, and covered with thick clouds. (*Works* 15, 330–31)

The illustration is striking for the manner in which it captures both the greatness of Christ and the small though significant beauty of every member of the church. Christ is the sun in Edwards's mind, the light which beams over all the creation. The saints are the tiny "drops" of moisture. Just as the sun's rays catch each drop, however small or insignificant, so does the love of Christ extend to each of His children. This light beautifies each person, each "drop," allowing each the opportunity to participate in the reflection of the Lord's loveliness. The combined beauty of all the raindrops is greater still, for "the whole as united [is] together much more beautiful," just as the church possesses a special beauty as it shines in collective witness across all lands. The church in gathered form, then, is an aesthetic exhibit of beauty that receives and reflects light from heaven.

The Church as "Militant" but Undefeated

Edwards gave his doctrine of the church historical weight and depth in his unfinished masterpiece "History of the Work of Redemption." There he disclosed that the church was not only linked to Christ, but satisfied by Him, and a unified display of His glory. While in the world, the church was "militant." Attacked by Satan and his minions, the church faced great trial. Believers lived no easy existence, but often had to endure terrible opposition and difficulty. However, this reality did not dim the beauty of the church, but only intensified it. The militant church consistently overcame the persecution it faced, giving great glory to God and rendering it more beautiful than before. In one section of the work, Edwards wrote that the church's preservation:

IS STILL THE MORE EXCEEDING wonderful if we consider how often the church has been approaching to the brink of ruin, and the case seemed to [be] lost, and all hope gone; they seemed to be swallowed up. In the time of the old world when wickedness so prevailed, as that but one family was left, and yet God wonderfully appeared and overthrew the wicked world with a flood and preserved his church. And so at the Red Sea, when Pharaoh and his host thought they were quite sure of their prey, yet God appeared and destroyed them, and delivered his church. And so it was from time to time in the church of Israel, as has been shown. So under the heathen persecution [of the Christian church]. . . . after the darkest times of the church God has made his church most gloriously to flourish.

He closed the section by celebrating the sovereignty of God in the trials of the church:

IF SUCH A PRESERVATION of the church of God from the beginning of the world, hitherto attended with such circumstances, is not sufficient to show a divine hand in favor of it, what can be devised that would? But if this be from the divine hand, then God owns the church, and owns her religion, and owns that revelation and those Scriptures on which she is built; and so it will follow that their religion is the true religion or God's religion, and the Scriptures that they make their rule his Word. (*Works* 9, 449)

Though Edwards did not include the word "beauty" in this passage, it is clear that he viewed the persecuted but persevering church as an emblem of God's glory and beauty. Throughout the ages, in "the darkest times," the Lord allowed the people of God "most gloriously to flourish." History was full of instances in which an antichrist sought to destroy the people of God, who became living screens on which the faithfulness of God, the "divine hand" of the Lord, most clearly appeared. For Edwards, the perseverance and victory of the saints in all ages, empowered by God, revealed beyond a shadow of a doubt the church's otherworldly orientation. As with all the created order, the life of the church proved a medium in which the Lord could further showcase His majesty and exalt the Son who secured His people in the palm of His hand (John 10:27).

Because God authored it, the story of the church was not in Edwards's mind a weak or precarious one. Considerable forces and foes rose up throughout history to stamp out the light of Christ as carried by His people, but they never succeeded, and never would. The "divine hand" made the history of the people of God a strong and resilient one. The unflagging perseverance of God's people testified to the strength and beauty of the one who empowered them. The church was militant and besieged, but it was also strong and highly favored— the possession of God who by their courage in all eras displayed "most gloriously" the beauty of the sovereign.

The Many-Splendored Church

As we have seen, the church is not a building. It is not a structure that one must heat, an edifice that one must repair. The church of God is part of the "mystical body" of Christ. The people of God who form the church in all its rich diversity share the highest privilege known to mankind, that of participating in the beauty, joy, and goodness of the Lord, of being satisfied in Christ and giving Him satisfaction. So far from being a building or a religiously minded organization, the church embodies the Savior. Through the Spirit, Christ is present in His church as it marches on, militant in this world, triumphant in the next.

Pursuing Beauty

Realize Church Is Not a Building but a Living Fellowship

*T*his may seem a small matter, but it isn't. The church is
by no means a structure or edifice, but is the body of
Christ. The identity of a group of Christians is not tied to a
particular location, but to their faith in Christ. A better starting point would be to refer to the church as the people of God,
and a church building as just that—the building in which the
people meet.

The body of Christ is a physical entity. The church is an
incarnate, embodied manifestation of God's glory, love, and
mercy in the world (Romans 12:4–5). It is not only a spiritual
institution but a physical presence, a tangible testimony to the
existence and majesty of God. Where believers are gathered,
they form the church. This is true whether one's local church
(gathering of believers) is great or small. Wherever Christians
worship together, they form a living picture of God's character,
a visible demonstration of divine glory. Perhaps remembering
this will help us to transcend boredom and discouragement in
our times of meeting. Local fellowships of great and small size
alike share the mission of displaying God's glory and embody-
ing His love, mercy, and grace. In the kingdom of God, every
community of believers has great significance and purpose.

Furthermore, it is essential that Christians remember that they have a very specific identity. We are not another religious group, a mere gathering of people with a shared background and ideology. We are the called-out children of God who have the mission of loving and proclaiming Jesus Christ together (Matthew 18; 1 Corinthians 11; Hebrews 13). Membership with a local church is thus very important. Nowhere does the Bible commend "lone ranger" Christianity in which we act and live alone. We are called to fellowship together (Hebrews 10:25) and to bear one another's burdens and sorrows (Galatians 6:2). When one of our number sins grievously against the Lord, and refuses to repent, we must remove them from our community in order that the Lord's name not be tarnished (Matthew 18). Within this body, we need to submit to our deacons and elders and work with them for the furtherance of the gospel (1 Timothy 5). In these ways and many others, Christians are to purposefully participate in the body of Christ, experiencing the joy of local church fellowship with people committed to the Lord.

Esteem Every Christian as Beautiful in God's Sight

*E*dwards reminds us of the biblical reality that every Christian has immense value to God and may participate fully in the work of glorifying the Savior. All too often in Christian circles, we mimic the world in esteeming the "best and brightest" and passing over those with less apparent value. This is a shameful mistake, one that robs believers of their sense of worth and agency. Every believer is a "drop" of beauty in the great display of God's character and thus can use his or her spiritual gifts and natural abilities in the service of the church of Christ (1 Peter 2:9). Furthermore, every person, regardless of race or background, age or occupation, is equally beautiful and lovely to the Lord. The history of Christianity shows that all too often Christians have discriminated against fellow believers just as the world discriminates among itself. Wherever possible, Christians should work to visibly demonstrate the unity of the church by overcoming racial, social, and economic boundaries. The church of God was never meant to be homogeneous, but a tapestry of many colors that shows the world that the cross of Christ unifies mankind in a way that nothing else will (Revelation 14:6, for example).

Let the Church Display Love Above All

*T*he church must preach the double-sided message of Christianity with boldness in the world, avoiding neither love nor judgment in its constant proclamation of the gospel. Yet the church's priority must always be love and grace. As the people who drink constantly from the love of God as the result of union with Christ through faith in His atoning death and life-giving resurrection, Christians must mark themselves as a grace-filled, love-giving people. Christians must not simply receive the greatness of God's love, as poignantly described by Edwards, but must imbibe it and present it to the world. The love of God, we must note, is biblically defined, and thus we must love the people in our lives along biblical lines, avoiding a more generic and less Christian brand of love (John 3:16). Our lives present us with countless opportunities to love the body of Christ and evidence a way of communal life that draws the attention of the lost and brings them into contact with an alien way of life (Matthew 5:16; 1 Peter 2:12).

Know that the Church Is Not Weak

Because the church is empowered by the "divine hand," Christians are not weak people, and the church is not a weak institution. Against all odds and appearances, the church of God can and will prevail over its persecutors, foes, and obstacles (Matthew 16:18). Every believer should live by such a view and every local church should operate according to this reality. Though outnumbered and outgunned, the church belongs to Christ and He sustains it with His own presence and power through union with believers in the Holy Spirit (Acts 1:8). This divine orientation renders us incredibly strong, despite appearances, and necessitates that we live and practice our faith with boldness and confidence in our sovereign God.

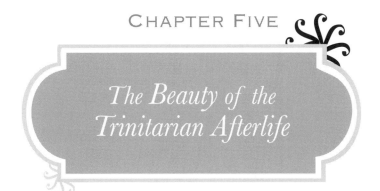

CHAPTER FIVE

The Beauty of the Trinitarian Afterlife

As noted in chapter one, the study of God begins in the dust. To think and speak of God requires a posture of humility, the recognition of one's finitude. As one lies in the dust, and the words of God roll over one's back, filling the air with the weight of holiness, one learns the truths of God and experiences the beauty of His presence. Such encounters transform us and leave us humbled and awestruck at what we have seen and heard. In certain instances, however, the believer is not laid low by God but lifted up. Like the old apostle John, who sat quietly in a prison cell far from his home in first-century Greece, the believer who searches the Scripture may suddenly catch a glimpse of another realm (Revelation 1 and following). In John's revelation and other places in Scripture, the believer sees a place where sickness and pain cannot invade, where streams of living water flow, and where the Lord reigns over all. The vision is brief and breathtaking, and it leaves the believer, with John, both stunned at the sight and stirred to press on until this new day dawns.

Throughout his life, Jonathan Edwards caught scripturally inspired glimpses of heaven. As he studied the Scripture and meditated on the age to come, he discovered "a world of love" where God, the fountain of beauty, lived with His beautified church in a cycle of mutual delight that filled all the heavens. Edwards, no stranger to sorrow and trouble in his life, often contemplated heaven and its joys. He found rich food for his soul in meditating on the realm where the Father, Son, and Spirit lived together in mutual happiness, and where the Christian could participate with the Godhead in the exchange of perfected joy. For Edwards, heaven was "a glorious loving society," a realm of beauty that shone with the fullness of the loveliness of God. Those who had seen the beauty and goodness of God displayed and reflected in the creation, who had found in the Son a pure ray of divine beauty, and who had themselves entered the society witnessing to God's excellence, now entered the realm from which all beauty flowed.

It is the purpose of this chapter to illuminate the nature of Trinitarian beauty as exchanged by the members of the Godhead in heaven and experienced by believers in that "world of love." Through study of his capstone Trinitarian sermon, "Discourse on the Trinity," this chapter will bring to light Edwards's unique understanding of the identities of the Trinitarian persons. The text will then cover the sermon "Heaven Is a World of Love," where Edwards developed the ways in which believers will share communion with the Godhead and participate in its exchange of love. In all, the believer will catch a vision of heaven and discover fresh desire for uninhibited communion with God in the life to come.

The Relationship Between the Members of the Trinity

Edwards began the "Discourse on the Trinity" by laying out the fundamental set of relationships between the persons of the Trinity. He wrote of the foundation of the Godhead that:

THE GODHEAD BEING THUS begotten by God's having an idea of himself and standing forth in a distinct subsistence or person in that idea, there proceeds a most pure act, and an infinitely holy and sweet energy arises between the Father and Son: for their love and joy is mutual, in mutually loving and delighting in each other. Proverbs 8:30, "I was daily his delight, rejoicing always before [him]." This is the eternal and most perfect and essential act of the divine nature, wherein the Godhead acts to an infinite degree and in the most perfect manner possible. The Deity becomes all act; the divine essence itself flows out and is as it were breathed forth in love and joy. So that the Godhead therein

stands forth in yet another manner of subsistence, and
there proceeds the third person in the Trinity, the Holy
Spirit, viz. the Deity in act: for there is no other act but the
act of the will. (*Works* 6, 121)

The Trinity takes its existence in Edwards's mind from "God's
having an idea of himself." This idea, as Edwards conceives it,
is the Son, the second person of the Trinity who personifies
God's perfect conception of Himself. The Father thinks about
Himself, imagining Himself as a person, and the Son is the
personification of this thought. The Spirit, the third person
of the Trinity, flows forth from both Father and Son "in
another manner of subsistence," proceeding from the first and
second persons as their "will." As Edwards understood them,
the persons of the Trinity shared life together in an unending
mutual exchange of love. The pastor outlined this idea in the
following passage:

WE MAY LEARN BY THE WORD of God that the Godhead
or the divine nature and essence does subsist in love. 1
John 4:8, "He that loveth not knoweth not God; for God is
love." In the context of which place I think it is plainly intimated to us that the Holy Spirit is that love, as in the 1 John
4:12–13: "If we love one another, God dwelleth in us, and
his love is perfected in us. Hereby know we that we dwell
in him, because he hath given us of his Spirit." 'Tis the same
argument in both verses: in the 1 John 4:12 the Apostle

argues that if we have love dwelling in [us], we have God dwelling in us; and in the 1 John 4:13 he clears the force of the argument by this, that love is God's Spirit. Seeing we have of God's Spirit dwelling [in us], we have God dwelling in [us]: supposing it as a thing granted and allowed, that God's Spirit is God. 'Tis evident also by this verse that God's dwelling in us, and his love—or the love that he hath or exerciseth—being in us, are the same thing. The same is intimated in the same manner in the last verses of the foregoing chapter. The Apostle was in the foregoing verses speaking of love as a sure sign of sincerity and our acceptance with God, beginning with the 1 John 4:18, and he sums up the argument thus in the last verse: "And hereby do we know that he abideth in us by the Spirit that [he] hath given us." (*Works* 6, 121–22)

According to Edwards, the "essence" of the Trinity was love. The ground and substance of interaction between the persons of the Godhead was transcendent affection and delight in one another. This bond of love proceeded from the inherent holiness of each of the Trinitarian persons and enabled them to enjoy one another without interruption or compromise. The Trinitarian love was of such strength that Edwards equated "God's dwelling in us" with "his love." To know God is to know His love, to drink from its constant flow, to experience the sweetness of life in the Spirit.

A "Society" or "Family"

Having sketched the essence of Trinitarian life, Edwards carefully defined the identities of the persons of the Godhead. All three members shared the majesty of divine being and each possessed the same traits, living together in a "society or family" characterized by perfect harmony. Each member, however, expressed these traits in different ways and with different functions:

HEREBY WE SEE HOW the Father is the fountain of the Godhead, and why when he is spoken of in Scripture he is so often, without any addition or distinction, called God; which has led some to think that he only was truly and properly God. Hereby we may see why, in the economy of the persons of the Trinity, the Father should sustain the dignity of the Deity; that the Father should have it as his office to uphold and maintain the rights of the Godhead, and should be God, not only by essence, but as it were by his economical office. Hereby is illustrated the doctrine of the Holy Ghost preceding both the Father and the Son. Hereby we see how that it is possible for the Son to be begotten by the Father, and the Holy Ghost to proceed from the Father and Son, and yet that all the persons should be co-eternal. Hereby we may more clearly understand the equality of the persons among themselves, and that they are every way equal in the society or family of the three. They are equal in honor besides the honor which is common to 'em all, viz. that they are all God; each has his peculiar honor in the society or family. They are equal not only in essence. The Father's honor is that he is as it were the author of perfect and infinite wisdom. The Son's honor is that he is that perfect and divine wisdom itself, the excellency of which is that from whence arises the honor of being the author or generator of it. The honor of the Father and the Son is that they are infinitely excellent, or that from them infinite excellency proceeds. But the honor of the Holy Ghost is equal, for he is that divine excellency and beauty itself. (*Works* 6, 135)

The concepts of *unity* and *diversity* are essential to understanding this passage. The Trinity is unified in that all its members share the essence of divinity. The Father, Son, and Spirit are all God, in other words, and each possesses all the entailments of being God. The members share a perfect harmony of soul that results from their divine unity. Though this may sound confusing, Edwards in fact gives us a very helpful metaphor by which to understand the Trinity, that of a family or society. The "family members" are united by sharing the essence of divinity.

At the same time, there is diversity within the Godhead, just as there is diversity within a family. As Edwards conceived of the family's roles, the Father issues a trait, like holiness; the Son, the exact image and idea of the Father, personifies this trait, being perfectly holy; the Spirit represents the expression of this trait from the Father and Son that emanates from the Godhead into the lives of believers, thus making them holy. In the Edwardsean view, each member of the Trinity has a distinct role to play in glorifying the Godhead and pouring this glory into the world. The diversity of the Godhead enhances the harmony of the family just as the different members of a family play different roles, or as the members of a symphony play different instruments in creating a symphonious and beautifully blended sound.

The love this family shares is so intense, so rich, that it spills out from heaven into the world. In the era of the church, when Christ has accomplished His redemptive mission, the Father and the Son send the Holy Spirit into the world to bring mankind into communion with them. The Holy Spirit brings the collective love and beauty of the Trinity to the hearts of sinners through the gospel. Where the gospel is received by faith, the Holy Spirit comes to dwell. In the following section, Edwards discusses how the Spirit unites the believer to the love of the Holy Trinity:

> IT IS A CONFIRMATION that the Holy Ghost is God's love and delight, because the saints' communion with God consists in their partaking of the Holy Ghost. The communion of saints is twofold: 'tis their communion with God, and communion with one another. 1 John 1:3, "That ye also may have fellowship with us: and truly our fellowship is with

the Father, and with his Son Jesus Christ." Communion is a common partaking of goods, either of excellency or happiness. So that when it is said the saints have communion or fellowship with the Father and with the Son, the meaning of it is that they partake with the Father and the Son of their good, which is either their excellency and glory— 2 Peter 1:4, "Ye are made partakers of the divine nature"; Hebrews 12:10, "That we might be partakers of his holiness"; John 17:22–23, "And the glory which thou hast given me I have given them; that may be one, even as we are one: I in them, and thou in me"— or of their joy and happiness, John 17:13, "That they may have my joy fulfilled in themselves." But the Holy Ghost, being the love and joy of God, is his beauty and happiness; and it is in our partaking of the same Holy Spirit that our communion with God consists. . . . In this also eminently consists our communion with the saints, that we drink into the same Spirit: this is the common excellency and joy and happiness in which they all are united; 'tis the bond of perfectness by which they are one in the Father and the Son, as the Father is in the Son, and [he in him]. (*Works* 6, 129–30)

The section is noteworthy for its helpful definition of a key term in this discussion, "communion," which Edwards defines as "a common partaking of goods, either of excellency or happiness." Christians who share communion with the Godhead "partake with the Father and the Son of their good, which is either their excellency and glory, or their "joy and happiness."

The Holy Spirit's indwelling presence, then, allows the believer to know in a personal way the "excellency or happiness" of the Trinity and to taste, accordingly, "the love and joy of God" and the "beauty and happiness" of the divine. Salvation, then, means that the believer enters a stream of divine love and beauty that sweeps them into the boundless pool of Trinitarian happiness. In a way that is difficult to comprehend but refreshing to contemplate, believers will in heaven drink unendingly from Trinitarian goodness and experience eternal delight in their communion, or fellowship, with the Godhead. Much more than earthly fellowship, heavenly communion will allow the believer to "partake," or experience in the most intimate and involved way, the beauty of God.

The "World of Love"

Armed with a basic grasp of the workings of the Trinity and the believer's participation in its relationship of love, we look now at Edwards's meditation on heaven in his unforgettable sermon "Heaven Is a World of Love." While Edwards covers the identities and roles of the Godhead in heaven, he devotes special attention to the nature of heaven itself. Early in the sermon he lays out his basic conception of heaven as the dwelling place of God:

Heaven is a part of the creation which God has built for this end, to be the place of his glorious presence. And it is his abode forever. Here he will dwell and gloriously manifest himself to eternity. And this renders heaven a world of love; for God is the fountain of love, as the sun is the fountain of light. And therefore the glorious presence of God in heaven fills heaven with love, as the sun placed in the midst of the hemisphere in a clear day fills the world with light. The Apostle tells us that God is love, 1 John 4:8. And therefore seeing he is an infinite Being, it follows that he is an infinite fountain of love. Seeing he is an all-sufficient Being, it follows that he is a full and overflowing and an inexhaustible fountain of love. Seeing he is an unchangeable and eternal Being, he is an unchangeable and eternal source of love. There even in heaven dwells that God from whom every stream of holy love, yea, every drop that is or ever was proceeds.

Edwards sketched out the interplay of love between Father, Son, and Spirit in heaven, showing how the Godhead's "infinite fountain" poured out its love in the world above:

THERE DWELLS GOD THE FATHER, and so the Son, who are united in infinitely dear and incomprehensible mutual love. There dwells God the Father, who is the Father of mercies, and so the Father of love, who so loved the world that he gave his only begotten Son, that whosoever believeth in him should not perish, but have everlasting life [John 3:16]. There dwells Jesus Christ, the Lamb of God, the Prince of peace and love, who so loved the world that he shed his blood, and poured out his soul unto death for it. There dwells the Mediator, by whom all God's love is expressed to the saints, by whom the fruits of it have been purchased, and through whom they are communicated, and through whom love is imparted to the hearts of all the church. There Christ dwells in both his natures, his human and divine, sitting with the Father in the same throne. There is the Holy Spirit, the spirit of divine love, in whom the very essence of God, as it were, all flows out or is breathed forth in love, and by whose immediate influence all holy love is shed abroad in the hearts of all the church [cf. Romans 5:5]. There in heaven this fountain of love, this eternal three in one, is set open without any obstacle to hinder access to it. There this glorious God is manifested and shines forth in full glory, in beams of love; there the fountain overflows in streams and rivers of love and delight, enough for all to drink at, and to swim in, yea, so as to overflow the world as it were with a deluge of love. (*Works* 8, 369–70)

Heaven, in Edwards's mind, is most fundamentally a realm of love. The Father, Son, and Spirit reign in heaven, loving one another and sharing their love "without any obstacle to hinder access to it." The human heart, created to thirst after love, finds its ultimate satisfaction in heaven. On earth, the Christian tastes love for a time, but the delight is quickly interrupted by one's sins and troubles. In addition, Satan is a powerful force in this realm, and he carries out a campaign of terror that desperately tries to undermine the communication of God's love to His people (see Job 1, for example). In heaven, however, neither sin nor Satan have a place. Only the Trinity lives and acts there. The happy "streams" and "rivers" of love "overflow" that world and overwhelm the senses. The moments of happiness that sprinkle us on this earth will one day give way to an eternal "deluge of love" that flows from the Godhead to our souls without end or interruption.

This love had a definite object, an end, which is God, in Edwards's mind. For him, heaven was a world of love, and the center of this world was God. Though some define heaven in terms of experiences and pleasures, Edwards characterized the realm as most fundamentally the place where God reigns bright as a sun, drawing all eyes to gaze upon Him:

THE LOVE OF GOD FLOWS out towards Christ the Head, and through him to all his members, in whom they were beloved before the foundation of the world, and in whom his love was expressed towards them in time by his death and sufferings, and in their conversion and the great things God has done for them in this world, and is now fully manifested to them in heaven. And the saints and angels are secondarily the subjects of holy love, not as in whom love is as in an original seat, as light is in the sun which shines by its own light, but as it is in the planets which shine by reflecting the light of the sun. And this light is reflected in the first place and chiefly back to the sun itself.

The pastor detailed how God's people participated in this happy world:

AS GOD HAS GIVEN the saints and angels love, so their love is chiefly exercised towards God, the fountain of it, as is most reasonable. They all love God with a supreme love. There is no enemy of God in heaven, but all love him as his children. They all are united with one mind to breathe forth their whole souls in love to their eternal Father, and to Jesus Christ, their common Head. Christ loves all his saints in heaven. His love flows out to his whole church there, and to every individual member of it; and they all with one heart and one soul, without any schism in the body, love their common Redeemer. Every heart is wedded to this spiritual husband. All rejoice in him, the angels concurring. And the angels and saints all love one another. All that glorious society are sincerely united. There is no secret or open enemy among them; not one heart but is full of love, nor one person who is not beloved. As they are all lovely, so all

> see each other's loveliness with answerable delight and
> complacence. Everyone there loves every other inhabitant
> of heaven whom he sees, and so he is mutually beloved by
> everyone. (*Works* 8, 373–74)

Over against views of heaven that paint mainly sentimental scenes, Edwards declared that believers "all are united with one mind to breathe forth their whole souls in love to their eternal Father, and to Jesus Christ, their common Head." There, believers will not have to struggle to focus on God and devote themselves to Him as we do on earth. All the sin and strife that clouds our love for God here will melt away in heaven, and we will see God in His glory. Our hearts that we must continually stoke now will soar with delight. Just as the sight of an adorable baby or a beautiful vista causes our jaw to drop, the vision of God that we see in the next life will impel us to adore God and celebrate His beauty. Though we sometimes wrestle with our hopes for heaven—Will beloved pets be there? Will we grow bored in worship?—Edwards's biblically infused words focus us on the essential reality of heaven, the goodness and beauty of God, and remind us that we will be so enraptured by Him that everything else will pale in significance.

After sketching the identity and roles of the Trinity and covering the way in which the Trinity shared its communion with the church, Edwards offered his audience a powerful oration on the heavenly blessing that awaited the church. Sojourning now through a "great and terrible wilderness," we so often observe the "fading of the beauty" of everything that we love. The shadows of divine beauty on this earth must all give way to the forces of time. Only the people of God possess a beauty that does not fade. Only the church will enter a resting place where God will give to us unending "milk and honey":

AND ALL THIS IN A GARDEN of love, the Paradise of God, where everything has a cast of holy love, and everything conspires to promote and stir up love, and nothing to interrupt its exercises; where everything is fitted by an all-wise God for the enjoyment of love under the greatest advantages. And all this shall be without any fading of the beauty of the objects beloved, or any decaying of love in the lover, and any satiety in the faculty which enjoys love. O! what tranquility may we conclude there is in such a world as this! Who can express the sweetness of this peace? What a calm is this, what a heaven of rest is here to arrive at after persons have gone through a world of storms and tempests, a world of pride, and selfishness, and envy, and malice, and scorn, and contempt, and contention and war? What a Canaan of rest, a land flowing with milk and honey to come to after one has gone through a great and terrible wilderness, full of spiteful and poisonous serpents, where no rest could be found? What joy may we conclude springs up in the hearts of the saints after they have passed their wearisome pilgrimage to be brought to such a paradise? Here is joy unspeakable indeed; here is humble, holy, divine joy in its perfection. Love is a sweet principle, especially divine love. It is a spring of sweetness.

Love could not flow as a "spring" only, however. It would grow and grow:

BUT HERE THE SPRING shall become a river, and an ocean. All shall stand about the God of glory, the fountain of love, as it were opening their bosoms to be filled with those effusions of love which are poured forth from thence, as the flowers on the earth in a pleasant spring day open their bosoms to the sun to be filled with his warmth and light, and to flourish in beauty and fragrancy by his rays. Every saint is as a flower in the garden of God, and holy love is the fragrancy and sweet odor which they all send forth, and with which they fill that paradise. Every saint there is as a note in a concert of music which sweetly harmonizes with every other note, and all together employed wholly in praising God and the Lamb; and so all helping one another to their utmost to express their love of the whole society to the glorious Father and Head of it, and to pour back love into the fountain of love, whence they are supplied and filled with love and with glory. And thus they will live and thus they will reign in love, and in that godlike joy which

is the blessed fruit of it, such as eye hath not seen, nor ear
heard, nor hath ever entered into the heart of any in this
world to conceive [cf. 1 Corinthians 2:9]. And thus they will
live and reign forever and ever. (*Works* 8, 385–86)

Emanating from heaven, the Edwardsean cycle of beauty
spans the created realm and returns to heaven. The cycle that
began with God returns to Him as the church, the possession
of the Son, joins the angels to express "to their utmost" their
love "to the glorious Father and Head of it." Divided on earth,
where unity is precarious, the church gathers for eternity in
heaven to commune with God and experience the fullness of
His beauty. No discordance or disharmony can be heard
there; all is a "concert of music" that plays a symphony of adoration. No darkness will fall there; only the "warmth and light"
of almighty God will exist in heaven. Every sense, every
second of thought, every intention of the heart, will focus on
God and His beauty. "The fountain of love" from God will
overflow, and the saints will always drink of that love, even as
they pour out their own love to God.

Heaven's Triune Beauty

So closes our study of the Trinitarian afterlife, the future
dwelling place of the church. We end much like the apostle
John after he received his revelational vision of heaven—
awestruck at what we have seen, captivated by the hope of
that realm, yearning for beauty and love that does not fade or

wane. We are comforted by the knowledge that we will soon be there. In the blink of an eye, we will see the Lord. We will join with our guides and teachers, with holy saints of old, with fellow servants like Jonathan Edwards, and we will worship the God of glory, tasting His love, savoring His goodness, and participating for eternity in the cycle of beauty.

 *Pursuing Beauty*

Study and Worship the Trinity

*T*he first order of application for most of us is this—to make contemplation of the Trinity a part of our spiritual lives. Many of us affirm the existence of the Trinity but go for years without studying it. Many of our churches, unfortunately, do little to help us in this area. We will never fully understand it, of course, but merely beginning to study it will greatly help us to comprehend the magnificence and multifaceted beauty of the Godhead. Many of us are captivated instead by paltry, shallow things because we have been fed a diet of fluffy media and airy preaching and spend very little time and energy looking into transcendent realities. Yet if we will allow it to do so, the Trinity as laid out in Scripture will blow our socks off. Let us work to address and change this situation and study the doctrine of the Trinity in the Bible. Books like Bruce Ware's *Father, Son, and Holy Spirit* (Crossway,

2005) and Robert Letham's *The Holy Trinity* (P & R, 2004) will help us to do so and to worship the Trinity with knowledge and insight.

Beware of Loving the World

*I*n a fragmented, busy, technologically infused world, it can be easy to fall in love with our possessions and material comforts. Edwards's view of the Trinity and of heaven reminds us, however, that there is a greater love to be had, one that does not weather and fade. As chapter two discussed, God has filled the world with His goodness and beauty. We do well to act on this truth. But we must take care that we love the Lord far more than we love our things, our friends, or even our families. It will be a challenge, but our central task in this life is to make our lives radically God-centered. This is no grim or joyless endeavor, but a spiritual enterprise that will consume us, satisfy us, and save our souls.

Seek Trinitarian Love Above All

*T*he fact that heaven is a "world of love" as Edwards put it must inspire us to love God on earth in order that we might love God in heaven. We should use Edwards's spellbinding picture of heaven as a motivation for holy living (see Colossians 3:1–10). Our reward awaits us. Though our journey to the other side involves sacrifice and hardship, all our effort to honor the Lord through the power of the Spirit will prove worthwhile in heaven. Knowing that we will live in a sea of love in heaven should inspire us to avoid the cesspools of sin that tempt us here. On this earth and in this day, love is often equated with extramarital sexual gratification and the sudden rush of emotion it brings. If we do not cultivate our love for the Trinitarian God, we will find ourselves weak when tempted by this momentarily satisfying vision of "love." But if we constantly remember the great flood of love that we taste now and will experience for all eternity, we will find ourselves able to regularly evade the fleeting pleasures of this world.

Define Heaven in Biblical Terms

*W*e must avoid a very common mistake in our human-centered age and avoid defining heaven by our terms. Just as God is not who we want Him to be, heaven does not order itself according to our tastes. We must not think that because it is a realm of pure love and happiness, it will reflect our conceptions of the same. Just because a pet, a house, or a sport brings us joy, for example, does not necessitate their presence in heaven. Though even Christians struggle to understand this, the greatest good and highest beauty we will find is God. Pets and homes and sports are great, but they do not begin to approach the greatness and loveliness of God. God is the gift we seek; He is the beauty we covet. He, and no other, will make heaven all that Scripture promises it to be (see Revelation 21–22).

*Beauty
Remembered*

*W*ith our study of the cycle of beauty concluded, we are
left with some final, Edwardsean thoughts on the
nature of beauty as it relates to the doctrine of God. The study
of the radically God-centered nature of Edwards's thought
transforms our understanding of God and of beauty even as it
shows us that the study of one is truly the study of the other.
To study God is necessarily to study beauty; to study beauty
is necessarily to study God.

This leads us to the matter of evangelism. All around us,
people are fascinated by beauty. They chase after it in art gal-
leries, reality TV shows, pageants, high school halls, and most
everywhere that one can go. Beauty, whether God-centered

or not, captivates the human mind and heart. Informed by our study of Edwards's writings, we can ask our non-Christian friends, "Can we study beauty without studying God?" Is it possible to study a subject freighted with transcendence without any reference to *the* Transcendent? It seems unlikely. To non-Christian friends, then, Christians should ask evangelistic questions of this sort and help people to discover the source of beauty.

The Edwardsean perspective on beauty also leads us to ask questions to ourselves and fellow Christians. To those who love to study the Lord and His truth, we must ask, can we study God without studying beauty? In countering an overly emotional and sometimes illogical culture, we Christians should not make the past mistake of ceding art, for example, to lost people. But if our God is beautiful, then we are by definition interested in beauty, as Edwards has shown us. The gospel does not shut down our imagination or our love for beautiful things, but rather fires and fuels them and directs them to the God who embodies beauty. No analogy, image, or description is sufficient to contain His excellence. He is light, and truth, and goodness. He is holy. He is altogether beautiful. All of our study of God, all of our doctrinal devotion, leads not to dead-end dogma but speeds us along a one-way street to worship of the living God. As we study the Scripture and experience the power of the Spirit-filled life, the beauty of the Lord shines out, and our hearts and minds do not simply learn *about* God, but increasingly adore, treasure, and exalt our great God.

Indeed, when finite beings like us look into the multifaceted prism of God's beauty, we find Him growing large even as we grow small. God, and not our concerns or demands, looms large. His beauty, displayed in the Word, nature, Christ, the church, and heaven shatters our man-centered conceptions of the same. God has made His world beautiful, but the glory of this realm is not its own. All that we see that is beautiful points us to a greater figure in a higher realm.

Until our hearts are finally freed of the chains of sin and narcissism, it is our daily duty to follow the words of the apostle Paul in Colossians 3:1, which relate so closely to the subject of this book and the aim of this series: "Set your minds on things that are above, not on things that are on earth." More than repaired self-esteem, more than pain-free lives, more than anything we can imagine, we need more of God, more of the things of Him, more of His Word and His Spirit, more of His peace, more of His joy—in order that we, growing more beautiful, might give Him more of the glory that He, being beauty itself, deserves.

Acknowledgments

*W*e have a number of people to thank for the production of this volume.

We would like to thank Dave DeWit of Moody Publishers. Dave is an excellent editor and has been a tremendous help and encouragement in all aspects of the process. It was Dave who suggested that this project encompass not one book, but five, forming a comprehensive and definitive introductory series. We are thankful for his vision. We would also thank Chris Reese, who gave excellent feedback on this and every manuscript and made each book clearer and better.

We would like to thank Dr. John Piper for graciously providing a series foreword. It is a signal honor to have Dr. Piper involved in this project. Dr. Piper has enriched our understanding of Jonathan Edwards as he has for countless people. We are thankful to the Lord for his ministry, and we deeply appreciate his commendation of this collection. We are thankful as well for the assistance of David Mathis, Executive Pastoral Assistant to Dr. Piper.

We would like to thank dear friends and family members who gave encouragement and counsel at various points in the project. To Bruce and Jodi Ware and the Ware family, thank you. Your support meant more than we can say.

Owen would like to thank his wife, Bethany Strachan, for her love. Bethany, I have no greater earthly gift than you. Your own beauty, seen from numerous angles, is an image of a greater reality.

Doug would like to thank his parents-in-law, Homer and Tena Hamster, to whom he dedicates this book in love and gratitude.

Above all others, we thank our great God, the embodiment of beauty, the sustainer of the church, the Lord of heaven and earth.

Recommended Resources on Jonathan Edwards

*F*or the premier collection of Edwards's own writings, see *The Works of Jonathan Edwards*, vol. 1–26, Yale University Press. Access these works in their entirety free of charge at http://edwards.yale.edu.

For secondary sources, we recommend the following.

Introductory Reading

Byrd, James P. *Jonathan Edwards for Armchair Theologians.* Louisville, KY: Westminster John Knox Press, 2008.

McDermott, Gerald R. *Seeing God: Jonathan Edwards and Spiritual Discernment.* Vancouver: Regent College Publishing, 2000.

Nichols, Stephen A. *Jonathan Edwards: A Guided Tour of His Life and Thought.* Phillipsburg, NJ: Presbyterian & Reformed, 2001.

Storms, Sam. *Signs of the Spirit: An Interpretation of Jonathan Edwards' Religious Affections.* Wheaton, IL: Crossway Books, 2007.

Deeper Reading

Gura, Philip F. *Jonathan Edwards: America's Evangelical.* New York: Hill & Wang, 2005.

Kimnach, Wilson H., Kenneth P. Minkema, and Douglas A. Sweeney, eds. *The Sermons of Jonathan Edwards: A Reader.* New Haven: Yale University Press, 1999.

Lesser, M. X. *Reading Jonathan Edwards: An Annotated Bibliography in Three Parts, 1729–2005.* Grand Rapids: Eerdmans, 2008

Marsden, George. *Jonathan Edwards: A Life.* New Haven: Yale University Press, 2003.

McDermott, Gerald R., ed. *Understanding Jonathan Edwards: An Introduction to America's Theologian.* New York: Oxford University Press, 2009.

Moody, Josh. *The God-Centered Life: Insights from Jonathan Edwards for Today.* Vancouver: Regent College Publishing, 2007.

Murray, Iain H. *Jonathan Edwards: A New Biography.* Edinburgh: Banner of Truth Trust, 1987.

Piper, John. *God's Passion for His Glory: Living the Vision of Jonathan Edwards.* Wheaton, IL: Crossway Books, 1998.

———, and Justin Taylor, eds. *A God Entranced Vision of All Things: The Legacy of Jonathan Edwards.* Wheaton, IL: Crossway Books, 2004.

Smith, John E., Harry S. Stout, and Kenneth P. Minkema, eds. *A Jonathan Edwards Reader.* New Haven: Yale University Press, 1995.

Sweeney, Douglas A. *Jonathan Edwards and the Ministry of the Word: A Model of Faith and Thought.* Downers Grove, IL: InterVarsity Press, 2009.

BRINGING YOU THE TIMELESS CLASSICS
Classics

Selected for their enduring influence and timeless perspective …

Answers to Prayer
ISBN-13: 978-0-8024-5650-2

The Confessions
of St. Augustine
ISBN-13: 978-0-8024-5651-9

How to Pray
ISBN-13: 978-0-8024-5652-6

The Imitation of Christ
ISBN-13: 978-0-8024-5653-3

The Pilgrim's Progress
ISBN-13: 978-0-8024-5654-0

The True Vine
ISBN-13: 978-0-8024-5655-7

Power Through Prayer
ISBN-13: 978-0-8024-5662-5

The Christian's Secret
of a Happy Life
ISBN-13: 978-0-8024-5656-4

Hudson Taylor's
Spiritual Secret
ISBN-13: 978-0-8024-5658-8

MOODY
PUBLISHERS
MoodyClassics.com

BRINGING YOU THE TIMELESS CLASSICS
Classics

... these are key books that every believer on the journey of spiritual formation should read.

Holiness
ISBN-13: 978-0-8024-5455-3

Born Crucified
ISBN-13: 978-0-8024-5456-0

Names of God
ISBN-13: 978-0-8024-5856-8

The Overcoming Life
ISBN-13: 978-0-8024-5451-5

All of Grace
ISBN-13: 978-0-8024-5452-2

The Secret of Guidance
ISBN-13: 978-0-8024-5454-6

The Incomparable Christ
ISBN-13: 978-0-8024-5660-1

Orthodoxy
ISBN-13: 978-0-8024-5657-1

The Apostolic Fathers
ISBN-13: 978-0-8024-5659-5

MOODY
PUBLISHERS
MoodyClassics.com